EMOTIONAL ALCHEMY

A GUIDE TO BOOST YOUR EQ SKILLS

ELANGOVAN RADHAKRISHNAN

Made with ♥ on the Notion Press Platform
www.notionpress.com

To my dear mom R Parvathi,

Your love and wisdom have shaped my world in ways words cannot capture. Your endless support has been my foundation, and your grace my inspiration. Everything I am, I owe to you.

To my loving wife E. Sujatha,

Your presence is the melody that sweetens the tune of my life. Your love has been my guiding light, illuminating even the darkest paths. With you, every moment is a cherished memory.

And to my precious children, Sakthi Haritha E, Harmitha Vani E and Ragav Varshan E

You are the stars that light up my universe. Each day with you is a gift, a new adventure that I treasure. My love for you knows no bounds; you are my heart, my soul, and my greatest joy.

This book is dedicated to the unwavering love of my mom, the boundless support of my wife, and the infinite happiness brought by my children. You are my inspiration, my motivation, and my everything.

With all my love and gratitude,

Elangovan Radhakrishnan

Contents

Foreword

Emotional Alchemy : A Guide to Boost your EQ Skills

Welcome to a journey that dives into the heart of what makes us truly human: our emotions. In this book, we explore something fundamental yet often overlooked—emotional intelligence. You might wonder, what exactly is emotional intelligence? It's the ability to recognize and manage our feelings, as well as understand others' emotions. Why does this matter? Because in the tapestry of life, emotions are the colorful threads that weave our connections with others.

In these pages, you'll find practical wisdom. Think of it as a guidebook, not filled with complex theories, but with simple, everyday ways to understand and handle emotions better. We'll explore how knowing ourselves emotionally can lead to healthier relationships and a happier life.

This book isn't about complicated jargon or scientific theories. It's about you and me, and how we relate to one another. It's about making sense of those moments when we feel joy, sadness, or confusion, and how we can navigate those feelings with grace and understanding.

We live in a world where kindness and understanding can sometimes feel scarce. This book aims to change that. By understanding our emotions and those of the people around us, we can create a world that's a bit kinder, a bit more compassionate.

So, as you turn these pages, I invite you to bring your curiosity and an open heart. Embrace the stories, the simple exercises, and the insights shared here. Let's embark on this journey of emotional discovery together. By the end, my hope is that you not only understand emotions a bit better but also find yourself building deeper, more meaningful connections with the people in your life.

Warm regards,

Elangovan Radhakrishnan

First Edition: 2023

ISBN - 978-93-6012-975-0

Preface

Dear Reader,

Welcome to a world where emotions take center stage. This book, "Emotional Alchemy: Guide to Boost your EQ Skills" is more than just a collection of words—it's a heartfelt exploration of the human experience. In these pages, we unravel the mysteries of emotions and how they shape our lives.

Have you ever felt overwhelmed by your feelings, or struggled to understand why someone close to you acted a certain way? You're not alone. Emotions can be complex, but they're also beautiful threads in the tapestry of life. This book is your guide to understanding them, both yours and others'.

We've crafted this book in simple language, devoid of jargon, because we believe that everyone deserves to comprehend the profound world of emotions. You'll find stories that resonate with everyday life, practical tips to navigate emotional waters, and exercises to deepen your self-awareness.

By the end of this journey, we hope you'll not only grasp the essence of emotional intelligence but also find ways to apply it in your daily interactions. Whether you're seeking better relationships, improved self-awareness, or simply a more harmonious life, the principles of emotional intelligence can light your way.

Embrace this book with an open heart and a curious mind. Let the exploration begin. Together, let's uncover the power of emotions and embark on a transformative journey.

Warm regards,

Elangovan Radhakrishnan
First Edition: 2023
ISBN - 978-93-6012-975-0

Acknowledgements

Dear Esteemed Readers,

I pen down these words with a heart brimming with gratitude and humility. As the author of "Emotional Alchemy: Guide to Boost your EQ Skills" I want to express my heartfelt thanks to each one of you who embarked on this transformative journey within the pages of this book.

Authoring this book was a labor of love, and your presence on this expedition has given it purpose and meaning. Your dedication to exploring the depths of emotional intelligence, your willingness to engage with the exercises, and your openness to embracing change have inspired me beyond measure.

I am profoundly thankful for your trust in the wisdom shared within these sections. Your commitment to understanding and mastering your emotions not only enriches your life but contributes to a more empathetic and compassionate world. Your efforts to cultivate emotional intelligence ripple outward, touching the lives of those around you, fostering understanding, and nurturing harmonious relationships.

Remember, the journey of emotional intelligence is not confined to the pages of this book; it is a lifelong odyssey. I encourage you to continue exploring, learning, and growing. Each step you take in this direction not only enhances your own well-being but also adds to the collective emotional intelligence of humanity.

Once again, thank you for your time, your energy, and your dedication. May your newfound wisdom in emotional intelligence guide you toward a future filled with profound self-awareness, genuine connections, and a deep sense of fulfillment.

With heartfelt gratitude,

Elangovan Radhakrishnan - Author

Prologue

In the quiet corners of our hearts and the depths of our minds, emotions dance like flickering flames. They shape our days, color our experiences, and guide our choices. Welcome to the prologue of "Emotional Alchemy:A Guide to Boost your EQ Skills" where we embark on a profound journey into the very essence of what makes us human.

Imagine a world where understanding your feelings, and those of others, becomes as natural as breathing. In the pages that follow, we delve into the art and science of emotional intelligence. It's not just a skill; it's a beacon illuminating the path to deeper connections, better communication, and a more fulfilling life.

Through stories, exercises, and simple wisdom, this book aims to unravel the intricacies of emotions. We'll explore not just the highs of joy and love but also the depths of sadness and anger. By embracing the full spectrum of human emotions, we can learn, grow, and navigate the complexities of our inner worlds.

As you turn these pages, consider this book as a companion on your own emotional voyage. Together, let's unravel the mysteries, celebrate the wonders, and harness the power of Emotional Intelligence.

With Regards

Elangovan Radhakrishnan

CHAPTER ONE

INTRODUCTION

When I was in the hustle and bustle of my daily life, I found myself rushing from one commitment to another. Work, family, and various responsibilities consumed my days, leaving little time for introspection. It was not until a moment of self-reflection that I realized I had lost touch with my true self.

Amidst the tranquility of my farmland, I found myself under the vast expanse of the open sky and beautiful trees, I found myself pondering life's bigger questions and my own purpose within it.

Figure:1

I began journaling my thoughts and feelings. It was a liberating experience, as I poured my innermost thoughts onto the pages. I discovered my fears, hopes, and aspirations, which had long been buried beneath the chaos of everyday life.

Over time, I made self-reflection a daily practice. I set aside a few minutes each morning to meditate and explore my thoughts. I also started seeking feedback from trusted friends and mentors, learning to embrace constructive criticism as a means of personal growth.

As I delved deeper into self-awareness, I uncovered my strengths and weaknesses. I recognized patterns in my behavior and emotions, enabling me to make conscious choices that aligned with my values. I learned to celebrate my successes without arrogance and face my shortcomings with humility.

Through this journey, I discovered that self-awareness was not just about knowing myself; it was about understanding how I impacted the world around me. It improved my relationships, as I became more attuned to the needs and feelings of others. It also empowered me to set meaningful goals and pursue a life that was truly fulfilling.

In the end, my personal story of self-awareness was not just a journey of self-discovery but a transformation of how I interacted with the world. It reminded me that amidst life's chaos, taking time for self-reflection can lead to a deeper understanding of oneself and a more meaningful existence.

CHAPTER TWO

UNDERSTANDING EMOTIONS

"Happiness depends upon ourselves." - Aristotle

Have you ever thought about why our hearts feel so many different things? Our emotions are like a colorful, swirling world inside us. Sometimes we feel happy, sometimes sad, sometimes angry, and sometimes we love deeply, like a fragile flower.

Figure: 2

Welcome, my friend, to the amazing world of emotional intelligence. In this special journey called 'Understanding Feelings and Being Aware,' we will explore our emotions, accept them, and learn how powerful they can be.

Imagine walking through a misty place, surrounded by feelings. We will learn what it means to be human and understand why we feel the way we do. This journey is not just about watching; it is about discovering ourselves. In these pages, you will find the key to understanding your own feelings. You will learn about your emotions, what makes you upset, and what makes you happy. This is a personal journey to know yourself better, like a candle shining in the dark.

I am sharing this knowledge with you not to confuse you, but to make you stronger. As we learn about our feelings, I want you to join in. There are fun activities in this book to help you learn more about yourself. Together, we will learn how to handle stress, fear, and sad feelings.

But I see curiosity in your eyes. You want to know more, don't you? Let us talk about empathy, the ability to understand others' feelings. Do not worry; we will learn how to connect with people. We will learn to listen, really listen, to others. By doing this, we can create deep and lasting friendships.

In this journey, we will learn from great leaders who understand emotions. They do not lead by being bossy; they lead with kindness, inspiring their teams to be great. We will learn from them and discover how to make good decisions using our emotions.

But wait, there is more to learn. We will also find ways to solve problems by understanding emotions. We will learn how to deal with disagreements by understanding each other, making our relationships better.

As we finish our journey, remember that emotional intelligence is not just in this book. It is something we can use in every part of our lives, at school, with friends, and even when we are alone. It is like a magic power that helps us feel good and make others happy too.

So, my friend, let us take this journey together, hand in hand, heart to heart. Let us open the door to a world where emotions are not just things, we feel but something we understand and use to make our lives better. This is more than a book; it is a friend guiding you to understand your feelings. Let us start this amazing adventure of embracing emotional intelligence!

Come, join me, as we dance amidst the glittering tapestry of emotions, and together, we shall master the art of empathy and self-awareness.

Tips: Practice Empathy: Put yourself in the characters' shoes. Try to understand their emotions and motivations.

1.1 THE SCIENCE BEHIND EMOTIONS: EXPLORING THE PHYSIOLOGICAL AND PSYCHOLOGICAL ASPECTS OF EMOTIONS AND HOW THEY IMPACT OUR BEHAVIOR.

"Act as if what you do makes a difference. It does." - William James

Emotions - they are complex, mysterious, and intricately intertwined with our human experience. From the earliest days of human existence, emotions have played a crucial role in our survival and ability to thrive. They have guided our decisions, shaped our relationships, and influenced our behavior in both profound and subtle ways. But what exactly are emotions? How do they work? And why do they have such a powerful hold on us?

To utterly understand emotions, we must begin by delving into their roots - the physiological and psychological aspects that underpin them. Emotions are not simply abstract concepts or fleeting sensations; they are deeply rooted in our biology and psychology, creating a complex interplay between mind and body.

To grasp the science behind emotions, it is essential to explore the physiological aspects that contribute to their formation. The human brain, with its intricate network of billions of neurons, serves as the epicenter of our emotional experiences. Research has shown that specific regions in the brain, such as the amygdala and the prefrontal cortex, play integral roles in regulating and generating emotions.

The amygdala, located deep within the brain's temporal lobe, is responsible for processing and interpreting emotional stimuli. It acts as an alarm system, alerting us to potential threats and activating the body's stress response. When we encounter a potentially dangerous situation, the amygdala triggers a cascade of physiological changes, such as increased heart rate, elevated blood pressure, and heightened arousal. These bodily reactions prepare us for fight or flight, allowing us to respond swiftly to any perceived danger.

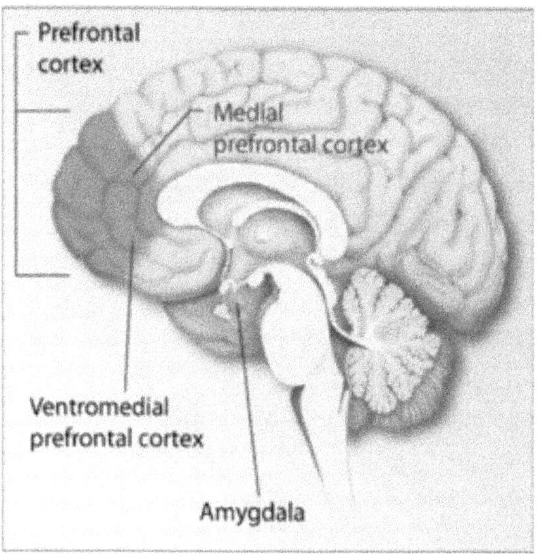

Figure: 3

In addition to the amygdala, the prefrontal cortex also exerts considerable influence over our emotions. This region, located in the frontal lobe, is responsible for regulating and modulating emotional responses. It helps us assess the situation, consider potential consequences, and make more reasoned decisions. The prefrontal cortex acts as a calming force, counterbalancing the amygdala's instinctual responses and allowing us to exert control over our emotional reactions.

But the physiological aspects of emotions extend beyond the brain. Our bodies are intricately connected to our emotional experiences through a complex web of neurotransmitters, hormones, and physiological responses. For example, the release of neurotransmitters such as dopamine and serotonin can influence our mood and overall emotional well-being. These chemicals play a key role in reward and pleasure systems, affecting our feelings of happiness, motivation, and satisfaction.

Furthermore, the intricate interplay between our thoughts, emotions, and physical sensations highlights the psychological aspect of emotions. Psychological theories of emotions emphasize the role of cognitive processes and subjective experiences in shaping our emotional landscape. According to one prominent theory, the cognitive appraisal theory, emotions are the result of our evaluation and interpretation of a given situation.

When we encounter a particular event or stimulus, our minds rapidly assess its significance, drawing upon past experiences, beliefs, and personal values. This cognitive appraisal then determines our emotional response. For example, if we perceive a situation as threatening or dangerous, we are likely to experience fear or anxiety. Conversely, if we interpret an event as pleasurable or rewarding, feelings of joy or excitement may arise.

The psychological aspect of emotions also extends to the influence of cultural and societal factors. Research has shown that emotions are not solely individual experiences; they are also shaped by the collective beliefs, norms, and values of a given culture. Different societies may prioritize and value certain emotions over others, leading to variations in emotional expression and regulation. For instance, in some cultures, the outward display of emotions may be encouraged and seen as a sign of authenticity, while in others, emotional restraint and self-control may be prized.

Understanding the intricate interplay between our physiology and psychology is crucial for mastering the art of empathy and self-awareness. By unraveling the complex web of emotions, we can gain a deeper understanding of ourselves and others, leading to more meaningful connections and enhanced emotional intelligence.

Emotions are not mere figments of our imagination or fleeting sensations. They are deeply rooted in our biology and psychology, shaping our experiences, and guiding our behavior. By exploring the physiological and psychological aspects of emotions, we can begin to unravel the mysteries of the human emotional landscape. Armed with this knowledge, we can navigate the intricate dance of emotions with greater empathy, self-awareness, and interconnectedness.

1.2 RECOGNIZING AND ACKNOWLEDGING EMOTIONS: THE IMPORTANCE OF IDENTIFYING AND ACCEPTING OUR EMOTIONS AS A KEY STEP TOWARDS EMOTIONAL INTELLIGENCE.

"The first step toward change is awareness. The second step is acceptance." - Nathaniel Branden

Emotional intelligence is a multi-faceted skill that encompasses our ability to recognize, understand, and manage our own emotions, as well as our capacity to empathize with others. It plays a crucial role in our personal and professional lives, influencing our relationships, decision-making, and overall well-being. However, before we can fully harness the power of emotional intelligence, we must first learn to recognize and acknowledge our own emotions.

The journey towards emotional intelligence begins with self-awareness. It is the foundation upon which all other aspects of emotional intelligence are built. Self-awareness is the ability to recognize and understand our own emotions and the impact they have on our thoughts, behavior, and relationships. It is about being present in the moment, aware of our own internal experiences, and in tune with our own emotional landscape.

Recognizing and acknowledging our emotions can be challenging. In a world that often emphasizes the need to suppress or ignore our feelings, it can feel counterintuitive to turn inward and confront the emotions that may be uncomfortable or difficult to face. However, it is precisely this act of recognition and acknowledgement that allows us to take control of our emotions and use them as valuable sources of information.

Research has shown that emotional suppression and denial can have detrimental effects on our mental and physical health. Bottling up our emotions not only leads to increased stress and anxiety, but it can also manifest as physical symptoms such as headaches, digestive problems, and sleep disturbances. By contrast, embracing our emotions, even the negative ones, can lead to greater emotional well-being.

The first step in recognizing and acknowledging our emotions is to cultivate a sense of mindfulness. Mindfulness is the practice of paying attention to the present moment without judgment. It is about observing our thoughts and feelings with curiosity and openness, rather than getting caught up in them. By practicing mindfulness, we can develop a greater awareness of our own emotions and better understand the triggers and patterns that influence our emotional responses.

Once we have become more mindful of our emotions, the next step is to acknowledge them without judgment or criticism. This means accepting that all emotions are valid and have a right to be heard. It is important to remember that there are no "good" or "bad" emotions – they are simply signals that something is happening within us. By acknowledging our emotions, we create a safe space for them to be expressed and processed.

Acknowledging our emotions also entails taking responsibility for them. It means recognizing that we are the sole owners and controllers of our emotions, and that we have the power to choose how we respond to them. Instead of blaming others or external circumstances for our emotional state, we can take proactive steps to manage our emotions in a healthy and constructive manner.

One effective technique for recognizing and acknowledging emotions is journaling. The act of putting our thoughts and feelings down on paper can help us gain clarity and perspective. By writing about our emotions, we can explore their underlying causes and discover patterns that may be influencing our behavior. Journaling also provides a safe outlet for expressing and processing our emotions, allowing us to release any pent-up feelings and make sense of our experiences.

Another powerful tool for recognizing and acknowledging emotions is self-reflection. Taking the time to reflect on our emotions and their origins can help us gain insight and develop a deeper understanding of ourselves. This can be done through meditation, contemplation, or engaging in meaningful conversations with trusted friends or therapists. By reflecting on our emotions, we can uncover hidden thoughts and beliefs that may be driving our emotional responses and make conscious choices about how we want to navigate our emotional landscape.

In addition to self-reflection, seeking feedback from others can also be instrumental in recognizing and acknowledging emotions. Loved ones, friends, and colleagues can offer valuable insights into our emotional behavior and patterns that we may not be aware of. By opening ourselves up to constructive feedback, we can gain a more comprehensive understanding of our emotional strengths and weaknesses, and work towards personal growth and development.

Recognizing and acknowledging our emotions is not a one-time event, but an ongoing process. As we continue to cultivate self-awareness and practice mindfulness, we become more attuned to our emotional cues and develop a greater sense of emotional intelligence. This allows us to make more informed decisions, build healthier relationships, and live a more fulfilling and balanced life.

In conclusion, recognizing and acknowledging our emotions is a crucial step towards mastering the art of empathy and self-awareness. It is through this process that we gain a deeper understanding of ourselves and others and pave the way towards emotional intelligence. By embracing our emotions and taking responsibility for them, we empower ourselves to navigate life's challenges with grace and authenticity. So, let us embark on this journey of self-discovery and emotional growth, and unlock the incredible power of emotional intelligence within us.

Tips: Reflect on Characters: Think about how characters handle emotions. What can you learn from their successes and mistakes?

1.3 EMOTIONAL TRIGGERS: UNDERSTANDING THE TRIGGERS THAT ELICIT SPECIFIC EMOTIONS AND LEARNING HOW TO MANAGE THEM EFFECTIVELY.

"It's not what happens to you, but how you react to it that matters." - Epictetus

Emotional triggers, those seemingly invisible force fields in our lives that can propel us into a state of intense emotional reactivity. They are like landmines scattered throughout our minds, waiting to be stepped on and detonated, igniting a surge of emotions within us. Understanding these triggers and learning how to manage them effectively is a crucial aspect of mastering empathy and self-awareness. In this section, we will delve into the depths of emotional triggers, exploring their origins, their impact on our emotions, and provide practical strategies to navigate through them with grace and control.

Figure:4

Our emotional triggers are deeply rooted in our past experiences, shaping our perceptions and reactions to present situations. They are like imprints from our past, etched onto our souls, reminding us of moments of pain, joy, or vulnerability. As we journey through life, we collect a mosaic of memories, each carrying its own emotional charge. Some memories are like gentle whispers, easily forgotten or dismissed. Others, however, linger within us like haunting echoes, waiting for the right trigger to bring them roaring back to life.

One of the first steps in understanding and managing our emotional triggers is to identify them. This requires self-reflection and a willingness to explore the raw terrain of our past. It can be an uncomfortable journey, as it forces us to confront parts of ourselves that we may have long buried or ignored. But it is through this process of excavation that we can gain insight into the origins of our triggers and begin to gain mastery over them.

My emotional triggers find their origins in the feeling of abandonment, a deep-rooted fear that surfaced after losing my father at the tender age of 7. This profound loss led to an overwhelming fear of abandonment, making me constantly apprehensive in my life. The slightest hint of distance or disconnection from loved ones would instantly trigger intense emotions, marking a struggle that began in my early childhood due to my father's absence

Once we have identified our emotional triggers, it is important to explore the specific emotions they elicit. Emotional triggers can provoke a wide range of emotions, from anger and sadness to joy and fear. Understanding these emotions and their underlying causes can provide valuable insights into our emotional landscape.

Take, for example, the trigger of rejection. When we feel rejected, we may experience an array of emotions such as sadness, anger, or even shame. These emotions are the result of our deep-rooted need for acceptance and belonging. When that need is threatened or unmet, our triggers are activated, and our emotions surge to the surface.

In order to effectively manage our emotional triggers, we must develop the ability to pause and reflect before reacting. This pause allows us to disengage from the automatic response triggered by our emotions and choose a more thoughtful and intentional reaction. This is not to say that we should suppress or ignore our emotions; rather, we should acknowledge them, examine their roots, and choose a response that aligns with our values and goals.

In the case of my trigger of abandonment, the pause allows me to take a step back and reflect on the situation objectively. It helps me separate the present moment from past experiences, allowing me to respond from a place of compassion and understanding, rather than reacting from a place of fear and insecurity.

There are several strategies we can employ to help manage our emotional triggers more effectively. One such strategy is mindfulness. Mindfulness practices, such as meditation or deep breathing exercises, can help us cultivate a sense of present-moment awareness. By focusing on our breath or observing our thoughts without judgment, we can create space between our triggers and our reactions. This space allows us to respond consciously and prevent ourselves from being swept away by the intensity of our emotions.

Another strategy is self-compassion. When we experience emotional triggers, it is easy to fall into a pattern of self-judgment or self-criticism. But by practicing self-compassion, we can offer ourselves kindness and understanding in moments of emotional turmoil. This gentle approach not only helps soothe our emotions but also encourages growth and resilience.

In addition to these strategies, it can be helpful to engage in therapeutic activities such as journaling or speaking with a trusted therapist. These practices provide a safe space for self-expression and exploration of our triggers, enabling us to gain deeper insight and heal from past wounds.

Mastering the art of empathy and self-awareness requires us to understand and manage our emotional triggers with care and finesse. It is a lifelong journey of self-discovery and growth. As we navigate through the mazes of our triggers, we come to realize that they do not define us; rather, they are the steppingstones towards greater self-compassion, understanding, and authentic connection with others.

Tips: Reflect on Characters: Think about how characters handle emotions. What can you learn from their successes and mistakes?

1.4 THE POWER OF EMOTIONAL AWARENESS: EXPLORING THE BENEFITS OF BEING EMOTIONALLY AWARE AND HOW IT ENHANCES OUR OVERALL WELL-BEING.

"The best and most beautiful things in the world cannot be seen or even touched - they must be felt with the heart." - Helen Keller

Exploring the concept of emotional intelligence and its impact on our overall well-being. Discussing the benefits of being emotionally aware and how it can lead to positive change in our lives.

Figure:5

To truly comprehend the essence of emotional intelligence, one must delve into its core components. The first building block is self-awareness, the ability to recognize and understand one's own emotions, thoughts, and behaviors. This self-reflection allows individuals to gain insight into their strengths, weaknesses, and personal triggers. By cultivating a deep understanding of oneself, one can navigate the intricacies of their emotions and reactions more effectively.

Equally crucial is self-regulation, the ability to manage and control one's emotions. It is the cornerstone of emotional intelligence, as it enables individuals to respond rather than react to various situations. Through self-regulation, individuals can maintain composure in the face of adversity, making clear and rational decisions. It is a skill that requires practice and discipline but yields immense benefits in terms of personal effectiveness and long-term success.

Empathy, the ability to understand and share the feelings of others, is another essential component of emotional intelligence. It is the bridge that connects individuals, fostering meaningful relationships and promoting a sense of unity. Empathy allows us to connect with others on a deeper level, to understand their perspectives and support them through their emotional journeys. It is a quality that enables us to be compassionate, tolerant, and accepting of the diversity of human experiences.

Lastly, but certainly not least, are social skills. These are the tools that facilitate effective communication, collaboration, and cooperation with others. Good social skills lay the foundation for positive interactions, creating a harmonious and productive environment in both personal and professional relationships. Whether it be active listening, conflict resolution, or networking, social skills enable us to navigate social dynamics with grace and ease.

The components of emotional intelligence are intricately intertwined, creating a holistic framework for understanding and managing emotions. If one component is lacking or underdeveloped, it can have significant implications for an individual's emotional well-being and interpersonal relationships. However, by actively working on these components, one can enhance their emotional intelligence and reap the countless benefits it bestows.

Research has shown that individuals with high emotional intelligence experience greater success in various aspects of life. They excel in leadership positions, as their ability to understand and connect with others fosters cooperation and inspires loyalty. They have a higher level of job satisfaction, as their self-awareness and self-regulation enable them to navigate stress and adversity with resilience and grace. They also have healthier personal relationships, as their empathy and social skills foster deeper connections and effective communication.

In today's fast-paced and interconnected world, emotional intelligence is more important than ever. It allows us to navigate the complexities of an ever-changing society, to adapt, and to thrive. By developing our emotional intelligence, we empower ourselves to make sound decisions, build meaningful relationships, and lead fulfilling lives.

So, how does one go about developing emotional intelligence? It begins with a commitment to self-improvement and a willingness to embark on an introspective journey. Start by cultivating self-awareness through journaling, mindfulness, and self-reflection. Take note of your emotions, thoughts, and behaviors, and seek patterns and triggers. Develop self-regulation skills by practicing mindfulness and stress management techniques such as deep breathing, meditation, or engaging in regular physical activity.

To foster empathy, engage in active listening and make a genuine effort to understand others‘ perspectives. Practice putting yourself in their shoes, and truly listen without judgment or interruption. Build your social skills by honing your communication skills, actively seeking feedback, and practicing effective conflict resolution techniques. Attend workshops, read books, or even take courses to deepen your understanding and refine your skills.

It is important to approach developing emotional intelligence as a lifelong journey. It takes time, effort, and a willingness to confront one's own shortcomings. But the rewards are immeasurable. By cultivating emotional intelligence, not only do we gain a deeper understanding of ourselves, but we also foster more meaningful and authentic connections with others. We become better equipped to navigate the myriad of emotions and challenges that life throws our way. We embrace our humanity and become the best versions of ourselves.

Take the first step and embark on this transformative journey. Open yourself up to the power of emotional intelligence and watch as your world expands and blossoms. The possibilities are limitless, and the benefits everlasting. Remember, emotional intelligence is not just a concept; it is a way of life, an ongoing commitment to growth and self-awareness. Embrace it and unlock your true potential.

1.5 EMOTIONAL INTELLIGENCE AND BEHAVIOR: EXAMINING THE CONNECTION BETWEEN EMOTIONAL INTELLIGENCE AND BEHAVIOR, AND HOW EMOTIONAL AWARENESS CAN LEAD TO POSITIVE CHANGE.

"Your emotions make you human. Even the unpleasant ones have a purpose. Don't lock them away. If you ignore them, they just get louder and angrier." - Sabaa Tahir

In recent years, researchers and psychologists have delved into the profound impact emotional intelligence has on behavior. People with high EQ are not just in tune with their emotions; they can also navigate complex social situations with grace and understanding. This understanding of one's own emotions forms the foundation upon which behavioral responses are built.

Figure:6

Emotional intelligence profoundly affects how people behave in various situations. Individuals with high EQ are better equipped to handle stressful encounters, exhibit patience in challenging circumstances, and express empathy towards others. They tend to be better communicators, resolving conflicts amicably and fostering positive relationships. By recognizing their emotions and understanding their impact, emotionally intelligent individuals respond thoughtfully, rather than reacting impulsively, thereby shaping their behavior positively.

Emotional awareness involves recognizing and understanding one's emotions, including their triggers and effects. This self-reflection is pivotal in altering negative behavior patterns. By acknowledging emotions without judgment, individuals can identify destructive habits and work towards change. This heightened emotional awareness acts as a catalyst for personal growth, allowing individuals to break free from harmful behavioral cycles.

Empathy, a key component of emotional intelligence, enables individuals to put themselves in others' shoes, fostering a deeper understanding of diverse perspectives and experiences. When people practice empathy, they become more patient, tolerant, and compassionate. This shift in attitude translates into positive behavioral changes, promoting kindness and understanding in relationships and communities.

Educational institutions, workplaces, and communities play pivotal roles in cultivating emotional intelligence. Schools can incorporate emotional intelligence training into their curricula, teaching children to recognize and manage their emotions from an early age. In workplaces, promoting a culture of emotional intelligence through leadership training and team-building exercises can enhance employee satisfaction and collaboration. Communities benefit from empathy-driven initiatives that promote understanding among diverse groups, fostering unity and harmony.

The connection between emotional intelligence and behavior is undeniable. By fostering emotional awareness, individuals can transform their actions and reactions, leading to positive change on a personal and societal level. As we continue to explore the depths of emotional intelligence, it becomes clear that a more emotionally aware world is a more compassionate, empathetic, and harmonious world, where positive change is not just a possibility but a reality.

CHAPTER THREE

DEVELOPING SELF-AWARENESS

"To thine own self be true, and it must follow, as the night the day, thou canst not then be false to any man." - William Shakespeare, Hamlet

Self-awareness stands as the foundation upon which emotional intelligence is built. We delve into the significant role of self-awareness in emotional intelligence, exploring its meaning, importance, and ways to cultivate it for personal and professional growth. Self-awareness is the ability to recognize and comprehend one's emotions, thoughts, and behaviors. It involves being in tune with your feelings and understanding why you feel a certain way. Self-aware individuals have a deep understanding of their strengths, weaknesses, values, and goals. They are conscious of their emotional triggers and can effectively manage their reactions in various situations.

Figure:7

2.1 THE JOURNEY OF SELF-DISCOVERY: GUIDING YOU THROUGH THE PROCESS OF SELF-REFLECTION AND INTROSPECTION TO GAIN A DEEPER UNDERSTANDING OF YOUR OWN EMOTIONS.

"The best way to find yourself is to lose yourself in the service of others." - Mahatma Gandhi

In the chaotic tapestry of modern life, the path to self-discovery is often obscured. "The Journey of Self-Discovery" serves as a guiding light, illuminating the way through the intricate realms of emotional intelligence. This book is not merely a guide; it is a companion, designed to help you embark on a profound expedition within yourself. Through the transformative power of emotional intelligence, you will learn to navigate the depths of your emotions, fostering a deeper understanding of the self.

Once, a group of three friends decided to go on a trek. They decided to hire a guide for the trek.

The guide was a very old man. He had an unkempt beard and long hair. He was very lean and walked with a stick.

The friends were surprised to see him. They thought he might not be able to complete the trek because of his age.

But, they were wrong. The old man was very knowledgeable and skillful. He led them through the trek with ease.

The friends were amazed by the guide's skills. They asked him the secret of his strength and endurance.

He replied, "I have been guiding trekkers for many years. I have gained a lot of experience and I have learned a lot from that experience.

"I have also practiced yoga and meditation for many years. This has helped me a lot."

The friends were impressed. They realized that the guide was a true leader who led by example.

They learned from him that a leader should always be open to learning and should always practice self-awareness and introspection.

Embarking on the Path of Self-Discovery

In the opening section, you are introduced to the transformative journey of self-discovery. This section emphasizes the importance of self-reflection and introspection in understanding your emotions. It lays the foundation for the practices and exercises that will follow, highlighting the significance of embracing your vulnerability and practicing self-compassion.

Cultivating Self-Awareness

In this section, a thorough exploration is conducted on the topic of self-awareness. It highlights how gaining an understanding of your emotions serves as the initial stage in discovering yourself. The section incorporates various techniques, including the practice of daily emotion journaling, where individuals can record their feelings, triggers, and responses. Additionally, mindful breathing exercises and body scans are introduced as methods to further develop emotional awareness.

Sample Practice: Daily Emotion Journaling

Set aside a few minutes each day to jot down your emotions. Describe what triggered these emotions and how they manifested physically. Reflect on any patterns you observe over time.

Embracing Vulnerability and Acceptance

The main focus of this section is to stress the significance of accepting vulnerability in order to explore your own identity. It highlights the transition towards embracing oneself and nurturing self-compassion. Additionally, it presents several techniques for engaging in mindful self-compassion exercises, which assist in fostering a more empathetic and supportive relationship with oneself.

Sample Practice: Loving-Kindness Meditation

Find a quiet space, close your eyes, and repeat phrases such as "May I be happy, may I be healthy, may I live with ease." Extend these wishes to yourself, loved ones, acquaintances, and even those you have conflicts with.

Exploring Core Beliefs and Values

This section explores how your core beliefs and values shape your emotions and actions. You will engage in exercises that help you identify their core beliefs and evaluate their alignment with your true self. Practical techniques, like the "Values Clarification" exercise, will guide in defining what truly matters to you.

Sample Practice: Values Clarification

Create a list of values such as honesty, kindness, or adventure. Rank them in order of importance to you. Reflect on how your daily actions align with these values and identify areas for adjustment.

Navigating Challenging Emotions

This section provides tools for dealing with challenging emotions, such as anger, fear, and sadness. Mindfulness-based stress reduction techniques and emotion-focused coping strategies are introduced. You will learn how to respond skillfully to difficult emotions without being overwhelmed.

Sample Practice: Mindful Breathing for Challenging Emotions

During moments of intense emotion, pause and take five deep breaths. Focus on your breath entering and leaving your body. Notice the physical sensations associated with the breath, grounding yourself in the present moment.

Building Resilience and Self-Compassion

This section focuses on building resilience through self-compassion. You will learn to bounce back from setbacks, embracing failures as opportunities for growth. This section includes practices like gratitude journaling and forgiveness exercises, fostering a sense of inner strength and self-love.

Sample Practice: Gratitude Journaling

Each day, write down three things for which you are grateful. Reflect on the positive aspects of your life, no matter how small they might seem. Cultivating gratitude enhances resilience and fosters a positive mindset.

Embracing the Ongoing Journey

In the concluding section, you are reminded that the journey of self-discovery is continuous and ever evolving. The section concludes with a reflection on the progress made and a call to continue practicing self-reflection and introspection in your daily live. The importance of integrating these practices into your routine for ongoing personal growth and emotional well-being is emphasized, leaving you inspired to continue your journey towards a deeper understanding of your own emotions.

Tips :

2.2 IDENTIFYING EMOTIONAL TRIGGERS: UNCOVERING THE TRIGGERS THAT CAUSE EMOTIONAL REACTIONS AND EXPLORING STRATEGIES TO MANAGE THEM EFFECTIVELY.

"The greatest glory in living lies not in never falling, but in rising every time we fall." - Nelson Mandela

Once, life was smooth sailing for me, until a friend asked, ‘Why do you react this way?’ Confused, I started a journey to know my feelings.

I met an old sailor who told a story about spotting storms early. Like a wise captain, he read signs in the wind and waves. I learned my triggers were like these signs — small things leading to big feelings. Understanding them was my guide.

Now, I can face rough times calmly. Just like that captain, I steer through life’s storms, stronger and braver.

Emotions are an integral part of being human, shaping our experiences and influencing our interactions. However, sometimes these emotions can be triggered by specific events, situations, or memories. We will delve into the fascinating world of emotional triggers, understanding what they are and how they impact us on a daily basis. Moreover, we will explore effective strategies to manage these triggers, enabling us to navigate our emotional landscape with grace and resilience.

Figure:8

Identifying Personal Triggers

This section delves into the personal realm of triggers. The "Trigger Journaling" exercise prompt you to jot down instances when you felt intense emotions. By detailing the triggering event, your emotions, and reactions, you will gain insights into your unique triggers. The section emphasizes the patterns that emerge, laying the foundation for effective management strategies.

Cognitive Behavioral Techniques for Triggers

Cognitive Behavioral Therapy (CBT) techniques take center stage. The section discusses the ABC Model (Activating events, Beliefs, and Consequences) and guide you in applying it to your triggers. Through practical exercises, you will learn to challenge irrational beliefs and reframe negative thoughts, reducing the impact of triggering events.

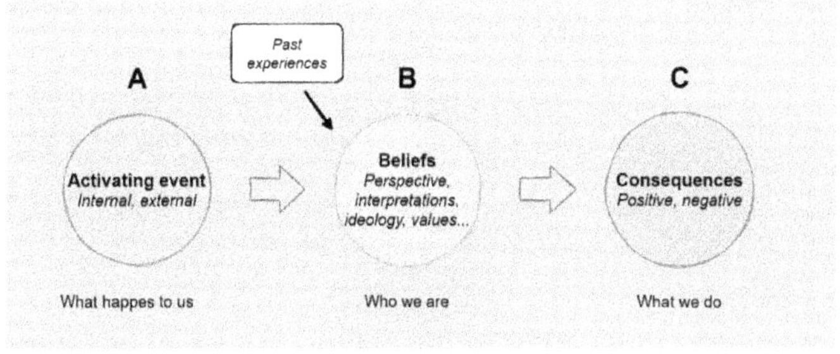

Figure:9

Mindfulness Practices for Trigger Management

This section explores mindfulness as a powerful tool for managing triggers. The "Mindful Trigger Observation" exercise encourages you to approach triggers with a mindful attitude. Through breath awareness and non judgmental observation, you will learn to respond consciously to triggers, breaking the automatic emotional reactions.

Emotion Regulation and Healthy Coping Strategies

The last section focuses on emotion regulation and healthy coping mechanisms. The "Emotion Regulation Toolkit" is introduced, comprising exercises such as deep breathing, progressive muscle relaxation, and visualization.

You are guided through these techniques, providing you with an array of practical tools to choose from when facing triggering situations.

Empowered Living Beyond Triggers

The conclusion reaffirms the importance of self-awareness and proactive management of triggers. You are encouraged to integrate the practices into your daily lives, creating a customized toolkit for managing triggers effectively. The section emphasizes the ongoing nature of this work and empowers you to continue your journey towards emotional resilience and well-being.

2.3 PATTERNS AND HABITS: EXAMINING RECURRING EMOTIONAL PATTERNS AND HABITS AND PROVIDING TECHNIQUES TO BREAK FREE FROM NEGATIVE CYCLES.

"Know thyself." - Socrates

Patterns and habits shape your life in profound ways. From the mundane routines of your daily life to the emotional patterns that govern your reactions, these recurring cycles can impact your overall well-being. In this section, we will delve into the realm of emotional patterns and habits, exploring their origins, their effects, and providing techniques to break free from negative cycles.

Figure:10

Exploring the Roots of Emotional Habits

This section focuses on the origins of emotional habits. You will explore the underlying beliefs and experiences shaping these habits. The "Root Cause Reflection" exercise guides you to journal about early memories and experiences related to their emotional patterns. By understanding the roots, readers gain clarity, enabling them to challenge and transform these habits effectively.

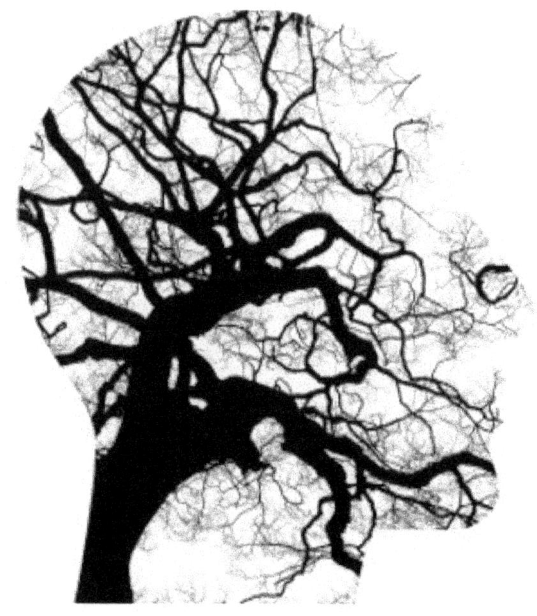

Figure:11

Breaking Negative Cycles Through Cognitive Restructuring

Cognitive restructuring takes center stage in this section. The discussion will revolve around challenging and reframing negative thought patterns. The section introduces the "Positive Affirmation Reinforcement" exercise, where you create personalized positive affirmations to counteract negative beliefs. Through consistent repetition, these affirmations empower you to challenge your habitual negative thinking. Pick few Positive affirmations which empower you.

Sl.NO	Negative Belief	POSITIVE AFFIRMATION
1	I'm not good enough.	**I am worthy of love and respect just as I am. I have unique qualities and strengths that make me enough**
2	I always fail	**I learn and grow from every experience, both successes and failures. Each setback is a steppingstone to my success**
3	I'm not capable of achieving my goals	**I am capable, strong, and determined. I have the skills and talents needed to achieve my goals, and I am making progress every day**
4	I don't deserve happiness	**I deserve to be happy, and I am worthy of all the joy and positivity life has to offer. I choose to embrace happiness in every moment**
5	I'll never be successful	**I define my own success. With determination, effort, and belief in myself, I create my path to success. I am capable of achieving my dreams**
6	I'm not lovable	**I am worthy of love and affection. I am lovable just as I am, and I attract positive and loving relationships into my life**
7	I'm constantly stressed and overwhelmed	**I choose peace over worry and calm over chaos. I handle challenges with grace and find moments of tranquility in every day**

Table:1

Mindfulness Practices for Breaking Emotional Habits

Mindfulness techniques are explored as powerful tools for breaking emotional habits. The section introduces the "Habitual Response Awareness" practice, where you will pause during triggering moments, observe their habitual emotional response, and then consciously choose a different, healthier reaction. By bringing mindful awareness to your automatic responses, you will gain control over your emotional habits.

Cultivating New, Positive Habits

This section focuses on cultivating positive emotional habits. You will learn strategies to reinforce new, healthier patterns. The "Gratitude and Positive Habit Journal" exercise encourages readers to daily jot down positive experiences and express gratitude. By consistently focusing on the positive, you reinforce their new emotional habits, creating a foundation for lasting change.

Embracing Emotional Freedom

The conclusion emphasizes the transformative journey you have undertaken in understanding and breaking free from your recurring emotional patterns. It reinforces the importance of continuous practice and self-compassion. You are encouraged to integrate the learned techniques into your daily life, empowering you to embrace emotional freedom and cultivate a more positive, fulfilling future.

2.4 EMBRACING VULNERABILITY: UNDERSTANDING THE POWER OF VULNERABILITY IN FOSTERING SELF-AWARENESS AND BUILDING AUTHENTIC CONNECTIONS WITH OTHERS.

"Vulnerability is the birthplace of innovation, creativity, and change." - Brené Brown

In a world that often values strength and self-reliance, embracing vulnerability may seem counterintuitive. However, beneath the surface lies a powerful tool for self-awareness and building genuine connections with others. you will explore the concept of vulnerability, its significance in personal growth, and how it can positively impact your relationships.

Vulnerability, at its core, is the willingness to expose your true self, embracing your imperfections, fears, and emotions. It involves stepping outside your comfort zones, breaking down walls, and allowing yourself to be seen authentically. By doing so, you will create space for growth and connection.

In this section, you will explore the concept of vulnerability as a source of strength. The discussion will revolve around understanding vulnerability as an essential component of authentic living. The section introduces the "Vulnerability Acceptance Meditation," a guided practice where you will sit in stillness, acknowledging your vulnerabilities without judgment. This meditation encourages self-compassion and fosters the courage to embrace vulnerability as a transformative force.

Vulnerability acceptance meditation is a mindfulness practice that focuses on embracing and accepting your vulnerabilities. It involves acknowledging and being open to the aspects of yourself that are usually kept hidden or protected. This practice draws from the principles of self-compassion and encourages you to cultivate a sense of acceptance and love towards your imperfections and vulnerabilities.

Here is how a vulnerability acceptance meditation session might be structured:

Set the Intention: Begin the meditation session by setting an intention. This could be something like, "I am open to embracing my vulnerabilities with acceptance and love."

Find a Comfortable Posture: Sit or lie down in a comfortable position. Close your eyes if you feel comfortable doing so. Take a few deep breaths to relax your body and mind.

Body Scan: Conduct a body scan to identify any areas of tension or discomfort. As you breathe, focus your attention on various parts of your body, releasing any tension you might be holding.

Acknowledge Vulnerabilities: Acknowledge the vulnerabilities or insecurities you feel. Allow them to come to the surface without judgment. Be aware of any emotions or thoughts that arise without trying to change them.

Practice Self-Compassion: Offer yourself words of kindness and understanding. You can say things like, "It's okay to feel vulnerable; it's a part of being human. I accept myself just as I am."

Visualize Embracing Vulnerabilities: Visualize yourself gently embracing your vulnerabilities. Imagine these aspects of yourself as delicate flowers or precious treasures. See yourself treating these vulnerabilities with care and tenderness.

Repeat Affirmations: Repeat affirmations related to vulnerability and acceptance. For example, "I am enough, just as I am. My vulnerabilities make me human, and I honor them with love."

Practice Gratitude: Conclude the meditation by expressing gratitude for your vulnerabilities. Consider how these aspects have shaped your experiences and contributed to your growth.

Return to the Present: Gradually bring your awareness back to the present moment. Wiggle your fingers and toes, take a few deep breaths, and when you're ready, open your eyes.

Unmasking Fear and Embracing Imperfections

This section focuses on dismantling the fear associated with vulnerability and embracing imperfections. The "Fear Deconstruction Journal" exercise guides readers to list their fears related to vulnerability and then challenge each fear with evidence to the contrary. By deconstructing fears, readers gain a realistic perspective, allowing them to confront vulnerability with resilience and authenticity.

Cultivating Self-Compassion in Vulnerable Moments

Self-compassion becomes a cornerstone in this section. The section discusses the practice of "Self-Compassionate Affirmations," where you will create affirmations emphasizing your worthiness and acceptance despite vulnerabilities. Through repetition and belief, these affirmations become a shield against self-criticism, enabling you to approach vulnerable situations with self-assurance and kindness. You can pick any affirmation from below.

1."It's okay to feel this way; my emotions are valid, and I am allowed to be vulnerable."

2."I am strong, even in my moments of vulnerability. My worth is not diminished by my challenges."

3."I extend kindness to myself in this moment of struggle. I am deserving of my own compassion."

4."I am not alone in my vulnerability; it is a shared human experience. I am connected to others through my challenges."

5."I treat myself with the same gentleness I would offer a dear friend in their time of need. I am my own source of comfort and support."

Authentic Connections Through Vulnerability

The focus shifts to building authentic connections with others through vulnerability. The section introduces the "Shared Vulnerability Exercise," encouraging you to open up to a trusted friend or partner about a vulnerability they have been hesitant to share. By witnessing acceptance and understanding, you will learn the transformative power of vulnerability in nurturing meaningful relationships.

Embracing Growth Through Vulnerability

The last section emphasizes the growth that stems from embracing vulnerability. The "Vulnerability and Growth

Journal" exercise prompts you to reflect on instances where vulnerability led to personal growth and self-discovery. By recognizing the positive outcomes of vulnerability, you are motivated to continue embracing it as a catalyst for your personal and emotional development.

The Liberating Journey of Embracing Vulnerability

The conclusion celebrates the transformative journey you have undertaken in embracing vulnerability. It reinforces the idea that vulnerability is not a weakness but a profound strength that fosters self-awareness and genuine connections. You are encouraged to continue practicing vulnerability, knowing that in your openness, they find the freedom to be authentically themselves and create deeply meaningful relationships with others.

2.5 THE ART OF SELF-REFLECTION: INTRODUCING VARIOUS METHODS OF SELF-REFLECTION AND JOURNALING TO ENHANCE SELF-AWARENESS AND PERSONAL GROWTH.

"The unexamined life is not worth living." - Socrates

In this section, you will explore the fundamental concept of self-reflection as a tool for self-discovery. The discussion will emphasize the importance of introspection in personal growth. The section introduces the "Daily Reflection Practice," encouraging you to set aside a few minutes each day to reflect on your thoughts, emotions, and experiences. This simple practice initiates the journey toward enhanced self-awareness.

Journaling for Self-Discovery

This section delves into the art of journaling as a means of self-reflection. You will learn about different journaling techniques, such as stream-of-consciousness writing and gratitude journaling. The section introduces the "Stream-of-Consciousness Journaling" exercise, where you will write continuously without worrying about grammar or structure. Through this practice, you will tap into your subconscious thoughts, gaining deeper insights into your inner world.

Visual Self-Reflection: The Power of Art and Creativity

Visual expression becomes the focus in this section. The discussion explores how art and creativity can serve as powerful mediums for self-reflection. The section introduces the "Visual Self-Portrait" exercise, where you will create a self-portrait using any artistic medium. This exercise promotes self-expression, allowing you to visually depict your emotions and self-perceptions, facilitating a deeper understanding of your identity.

The Visual Self-portrait exercise is a creative and introspective activity designed to help you explore your self-image, emotions, and inner identity. Here is how you can approach this exercise in the second person context:

Step 1: Gather Your Materials Start by gathering art supplies such as paper, pencils, markers, pastels, or any other artistic tools you prefer. Find a quiet and comfortable space where you can focus without distractions.

Step 2: Reflect on Your Feelings and Identity Take a moment to reflect on your emotions, experiences, and aspects of your identity you want to explore. Consider your strengths, challenges, aspirations, and how you perceive yourself.

Step 3: Begin Drawing Your Self-portrait With the materials ready, start drawing your self-portrait. Visualize how you want to represent yourself on paper. You can draw a realistic portrait or opt for an abstract representation that captures your emotions.

Step 4: Add Symbolism and Colors As you draw, consider adding symbols, colors, and elements that represent various aspects of your personality and emotions. For example, you might use warm colors to represent passion and energy or incorporate nature symbols to signify growth and renewal.

Step 5: Reflect on Your Creation Once your self-portrait is complete, take a moment to reflect on the choices you made. Consider why you chose specific colors, symbols, or expressions. Reflect on how your self-portrait represents your inner self and the emotions you wanted to convey.

Step 6: Write a Reflection Incorporate a written reflection alongside your visual self-portrait. Write about your experience during the creative process. Describe the emotions you felt, the symbolism you used, and what you learned about yourself through this exercise.

Step 7: Share and Discuss (Optional) If you feel comfortable, consider sharing your visual self-portrait and reflection with a trusted friend, therapist, or support group. Discussing your creation with others can provide valuable insights and deepen your self-awareness.

Nature and Mindful Self-Reflection

Connecting with nature becomes a unique avenue for self-reflection. The section discusses the practice of "Nature Walk Contemplation," where you will take a mindful walk-in nature, observing the natural surroundings and reflecting on how they relate to your own life. Engaging with nature in this way fosters a sense of interconnectedness, providing fresh perspectives on your personal challenges and growth.

Figure:12

Integrating Self-Reflection into Daily Life

This section focuses on integrating self-reflection seamlessly into daily routines. The section introduces the "Reflective Morning Routine," encouraging you to incorporate self-reflection practices, such as journaling or meditation, into their mornings. By starting the day with self-awareness, you will set a positive tone for the rest of your day, fostering continuous personal growth.

The Reflective Path to Self-Discovery

The conclusion reinforces the transformative power of self-reflection in the journey toward self-discovery and personal growth. It emphasizes that self-reflection is an ongoing practice, a lifelong journey of understanding you deeply. You are encouraged to embrace the various methods introduced in the book, knowing that through consistent self-reflection, they can navigate life with greater clarity, purpose, and self-awareness.

CHAPTER FOUR

MASTERING SELF-REGULATION

In my journey of mastering self-regulation, I faced a daunting challenge at work. A colleague and I clashed over a project, igniting my temper. Instead of reacting impulsively, I took a deep breath, pausing to understand my emotions. Through conscious effort, I channeled my frustration into constructive communication, addressing our concerns calmly. It wasn't easy, but by regulating my impulses, I defused the tension. Over time, this practice transformed not just my work relationships but my personal life too. I learned that by mastering self-regulation, I gained control over my reactions, fostering harmony in both professional and personal spheres.

In today's fast-paced and demanding world, the ability to self-regulate our emotions plays a crucial role in our overall well-being and success. Emotional intelligence, or EQ, is a valuable skill that can help us navigate through challenging situations and maintain a sense of balance. In this section, we will explore the concept of self-regulation and how it can be enhanced through the practice of emotional intelligence.

Figure:13

Understanding Self-Regulation

Self-regulation refers to our ability to manage and control your emotions, thoughts, and behaviors in order to adapt to different situations. It involves being aware of your emotions, understanding the impact, and effectively managing them. Through self-regulation, we can avoid impulsive reactions and make more thoughtful choices.

The Role of Emotional Intelligence

Emotional intelligence encompasses a set of skills that enable us to recognize, understand, and manage your own emotions, as well as understand and empathize with the emotions of others. It includes self-awareness, self-management, social awareness, and relationship management. By developing emotional intelligence, you can strengthen your self-regulation abilities.

Strategies for Enhancing Self-Regulation

1. Mindfulness: Practicing mindfulness can help increase self-awareness and enable us to observe our emotions without judgment. By being present in the moment and tuning into your feelings, you can better regulate your responses.

2. Stress management: Developing effective stress management techniques, such as deep breathing exercises, meditation, or engaging in physical activity, can help you cope with challenging situations and prevent emotional overload.

3. Cognitive reframing: Challenging negative thoughts and reframing them in a more positive or realistic light can help you to regulate your emotional responses. By shifting your perspective, you can maintain a more balanced outlook.

Cultivating Emotional Intelligence

1. Self-reflection: Taking time for self-reflection allows you to gain insights into your emotional patterns and triggers. Journaling, therapy, or seeking feedback from trusted individuals can aid in this process.

2. Empathy development: Practicing empathy and actively seeking to understand the emotions of others can enhance your ability to regulate your own emotions. By recognizing and validating the feelings of those around us, we can foster better relationships and build stronger emotional intelligence.

Mastering self-regulation through the lens of emotional intelligence is a powerful tool in our personal and professional lives. By understanding your emotions, managing stress, and developing empathy, you can navigate challenges with grace and achieve greater overall well-being. Let us embark on this journey of self-discovery and growth, harnessing the power of emotional intelligence to unlock your true potential.

3.1 THE IMPORTANCE OF SELF-REGULATION: EXPLORING THE BENEFITS OF EFFECTIVELY MANAGING EMOTIONS AND THE IMPACT IT HAS ON OUR WELL-BEING.

"The best way to predict your future is to create it." - Abraham Lincoln

In this section, you will explore the intricate relationship between emotions and self-regulation. The discussion emphasizes the impact emotions have on mental and physical well-being. The section introduces the "Emotion Awareness Meditation," guiding you to observe your emotions without judgment. This practice lays the foundation for understanding emotional triggers, a crucial step toward effective self-regulation.

The Science of Self-Regulation

This section delves into the neuroscience behind self-regulation. You will learn about the brain's role in managing emotions and impulse control. The section introduces the "Breath Control Exercise," where you will practice deep, controlled breathing to activate the body's relaxation response. This exercise demonstrates the physiological impact of self-regulation techniques, fostering a deeper understanding of their importance.

Breath control exercises, also known as breathing exercises or pranayama in the context of yoga, involve conscious manipulation of the breath. These exercises focus on regulating the breath patterns to promote relaxation, reduce stress, enhance focus, and improve overall well-being. Various breath control techniques have been practiced for centuries in different cultures and traditions.

Here are a few common breath control exercises:

Deep Breathing (Diaphragmatic Breathing):

•Sit or lie down in a comfortable position.

•Inhale deeply through your nose, allowing your lungs to fill with air. Feel your diaphragm expanding.

•Exhale slowly and completely through your mouth or nose, feeling your abdomen fall.

•Focus on making your inhales and exhales smooth, deep, and rhythmic.

•Repeat for several breath cycles.

4-7-8 Breathing:

•Inhale quietly through your nose to a mental count of 4.

•Hold your breath to a count of 7.

•Exhale completely and audibly through your mouth to a count of 8.

•This cycle represents one breath. Repeat for several cycles.

Alternate Nostril Breathing (Nadi Shodhana):

•Use your right thumb to close your right nostril and inhale deeply through your left nostril.

•Close your left nostril with your right ring finger, release your right nostril, and exhale completely.

•Inhale deeply through your right nostril.

•Close your right nostril again, release your left nostril, and exhale completely.

•This completes one cycle. Repeat for several cycles.

Belly Breathing (Abdominal Breathing):

•Place one hand on your chest and the other on your abdomen.

•Inhale deeply through your nose, allowing your diaphragm to expand and your abdomen to rise.

•Exhale completely through your mouth or nose, feeling your abdomen fall.

•Focus on making your breaths deep and centered in your abdomen.

Box Breathing:

•Inhale through your nose for a count of 4.

•Hold your breath for a count of 4.

•Exhale completely for a count of 4.

•Pause and hold your breath out for another count of 4.

•Repeat this cycle for several rounds.

Breath control exercises can be practiced at any time of the day, especially during moments of stress or when you need to relax and focus. Regular practice can enhance your overall respiratory health and promote a sense of calm and relaxation.

Emotional Intelligence and Self-Regulation

The focus shifts to emotional intelligence and its connection to self-regulation. The section explores the five components of emotional intelligence and how they contribute to effective emotion management. You will engage in the "Emotion Labeling Practice," where they identify and label their emotions accurately. This exercise enhances emotional awareness, a key element in self-regulation.

Emotion labeling practice, also known as affect labeling, is a psychological technique that involves identifying and labeling your emotions. This practice is based on the idea that putting your feelings into words can help you better understand and regulate your emotions. It is a mindfulness technique that encourages self-awareness and emotional intelligence. Here's how emotion labeling works:

1. Recognize Your Emotions: The first step is to become aware of what you are feeling. Pay attention to your emotional state without judgment. Are you feeling happy, sad, angry, anxious, or something else?

2. Identify the Emotion: Once you recognize the emotion, try to pinpoint it more specifically. For example, instead of just feeling "bad," you might realize that you are feeling frustrated, disappointed, or overwhelmed.

3. Put It into Words: Articulate your emotion by putting it into words. Say to yourself, "I am feeling [emotion]," or "I am [emotion] because of [reason]." For example, "I am feeling anxious because of the upcoming presentation," or "I am feeling joyful because I achieved my goal."

4. Validate Your Feelings: Acknowledge that your emotions are valid and normal human experiences. It is okay to feel the way you do, and labeling your emotions helps you accept and work through them.

5. Practice Non-Judgmental Awareness: As you label your emotions, try to do so without self-criticism. Avoid labeling your feelings as good or bad. Emotions are natural responses to situations and understanding them can lead to healthier responses.

Benefits of Emotion Labeling:

•Emotional Regulation: Labeling emotions helps you regulate them. By putting feelings into words, the emotional intensity often decreases.

•Improved Self-Awareness: It enhances your self-awareness by making you more conscious of your emotional responses.

•Better Communication: When you can clearly identify and express your emotions, it becomes easier to communicate with others about how you feel.

•Reduced Stress: Labeling emotions can reduce stress and anxiety by creating a sense of order and understanding in your mind.

By practicing emotion labeling regularly, you can develop a stronger connection with your emotions, leading to better emotional regulation and overall well-being.

Strategies for Enhancing Self-Regulation

This section offers practical strategies for enhancing self-regulation skills. You will learn about techniques such as mindfulness, cognitive reappraisal, and positive self-talk. The section introduces the "Mindful Body Scan," guiding you to focus their attention on various parts of your body, releasing tension and promoting relaxation. Through this practice, you will experience firsthand the calming effect of mindfulness on your emotional state.

Self-Regulation in Daily Life

This section explores the application of self-regulation in various aspects of daily life. The section discusses how self-regulation contributes to better decision-making, healthier relationships, and overall well-being. You will engage in the "Self-Regulated Decision Making" exercise, where they analyze a challenging decision using the STOP technique (Stop, take a Breath, Observe, Proceed). This exercise empowers you to apply self-regulation in real-life situations, enhancing your ability to respond thoughtfully rather than react impulsively.

The STOP technique is a mindfulness-based self-regulation exercise that can be highly effective in decision-making, especially during moments of stress or when strong emotions are involved. It helps individuals pause, step back, and make more thoughtful and rational decisions. Here is how you can apply the STOP technique for self-regulated decision-making:

S - Stop:

When faced with a decision-making situation, the first step is to stop physically and mentally. Pause whatever you are doing or thinking. Interrupt the automatic flow of your thoughts and actions.

T - Take a Breath:

Take a few slow, deep breaths. Focus your attention on the sensation of your breath entering and leaving your body. This helps to bring your awareness to the present moment and calms your nervous system.

O - Observe:

Observe your thoughts, emotions, and physical sensations without judgment. Acknowledge what you are thinking and feeling without trying to suppress or amplify these experiences. Be aware of any impulsive urges or emotional reactions.

P - Proceed Mindfully:

After taking a moment to observe your thoughts and emotions, proceed mindfully. Consider the decision you need to make and weigh the options. Think about the potential consequences of each option. Reflect on your values and long-term goals. Ask yourself what choice aligns best with your values and what will lead to the most positive outcomes.

Additional Tips:

Practice Non-Judgment: Avoid judging your thoughts or emotions as good or bad. Accept them as natural human experiences.

Consider Long-Term Consequences: Reflect on how your decision might impact your future self and others around you.

Use Positive Affirmations: Remind yourself of your strengths and capabilities, reinforcing your confidence in making decisions.

Seek Support: If the decision is significant, consider discussing it with a trusted friend, mentor, or therapist to gain different perspectives.

By practicing the STOP technique, you create a mental space between stimulus and response, allowing for more thoughtful and deliberate decision-making. This exercise enhances self-regulation by promoting self-awareness and giving you the opportunity to respond skillfully rather than react impulsively.

Cultivating Emotional Mastery and Well-Being

The conclusion emphasizes the transformative journey you have undertaken in understanding and applying self-regulation techniques. It reinforces that self-regulation is a skill that can be cultivated with practice and patience, leading to enhanced emotional mastery and overall well-being. You are encouraged to continue their self-regulation practices, knowing that by effectively managing your emotions, they can navigate life's challenges with resilience, grace, and inner peace.

3.2 STRESS MANAGEMENT TECHNIQUES: PROVIDING PRACTICAL STRATEGIES TO HANDLE STRESS AND ANXIETY THROUGH EMOTIONAL REGULATION.

"It's not the load that breaks you down, it's the way you carry it." - Lou Holtz

In this section, you will explore the concept of stress and its relationship with emotions. The discussion focuses on the impact of unregulated emotions on stress levels. The section introduces the "Emotion Awareness Exercise," guiding you to identify and label their emotions when they feel stressed. This practice lays the foundation for understanding the connection between emotions and stress, a vital step toward effective stress management.

Mindfulness-Based Stress Reduction

This section delves into mindfulness as a powerful tool for stress management. You will learn about Mindfulness-

Based Stress Reduction (MBSR) techniques and their effectiveness in reducing stress and anxiety. The section introduces the "Body Scan Meditation," a guided practice where you will systematically focus on various parts of their body, promoting relaxation and stress relief. Through this exercise, you will experience the calming effect of mindfulness on your overall well-being.

Cognitive Restructuring for Stressful Situations

The focus shifts to cognitive restructuring techniques. The section explores how changing negative thought patterns can alleviate stress. You will engage in the "Stressful Situation Reframing" exercise, where they identify, and challenge negative thoughts associated with a stressful situation. By reframing these thoughts, you will gain a more balanced perspective, reducing the emotional impact of stressors.

Stressful situation reframing, also known as cognitive reframing or cognitive restructuring, is a psychological technique used to change the way you perceive and interprets a stressful situation. The goal is to shift negative thought patterns and beliefs into more positive, empowering, or realistic perspectives. By reframing, you can reduce emotional distress and improve their ability to cope with challenging situations.

Here's how stressful situation reframing works:

1. Identify Negative Thoughts: Start by recognizing the negative thoughts or beliefs you have about a specific stressful situation. These thoughts often contribute to feelings of anxiety, frustration, or helplessness.

2. Challenge Negative Thoughts: Examine the validity of your negative thoughts. Ask yourself if there is evidence to support these thoughts. Often, our initial reactions are influenced by cognitive biases or automatic negative

thinking. Challenge these thoughts with objective evidence.

3. Find Alternative Interpretations: Once you have challenged the negative thoughts, try to find alternative, more balanced, or positive interpretations of the situation. Consider different perspectives or angles that you might not have initially thought about.

4. Practice Positive Self-Talk: Replace negative self-talk with positive affirmations and encouraging statements. For example, replace "I can't handle this" with "I can handle this, one step at a time."

5. Reframe Catastrophizing: If you tend to catastrophize situations (imagine the worst possible outcomes), consciously challenge these catastrophic thoughts. Consider the likelihood of the worst-case scenario happening and think about more realistic outcomes.

6. Consider the Learning Opportunity: Reframe the situation as a learning opportunity. Ask yourself what you can learn from this experience or how it can contribute to your personal growth.

7. Practice Gratitude: Focus on aspects of the situation or your life for which you are grateful. Shifting your focus to positive aspects can change your overall perspective on the situation.

8. Seek Support: Talk to a trusted friend, family member, or mental health professional about the situation. They might offer different viewpoints or insights that can help you reframe your perspective.

Benefits of Stressful Situation Reframing:

Reduces anxiety and stress.

Enhances problem-solving skills.

Improves emotional regulation.

Boosts resilience and coping abilities.

Promotes a more optimistic outlook on life.

By reframing stressful situations, individuals can build psychological resilience and navigate challenges with a more positive mindset, leading to improved overall well-being.

Building Resilience Through Emotional Intelligence

The last section explores the role of emotional intelligence in building resilience against stress. The section discusses empathy, self-awareness, and interpersonal relationships as essential components of emotional intelligence. You will engage in the "Empathy Practice," where you actively listen to a friend or family member, aiming to understand your emotions and perspectives. By cultivating empathy, you will enhance your emotional intelligence, enabling you to navigate stressful situations with greater understanding and composure.

Empathy practice involves the intentional effort to understand and share the feelings, thoughts, and perspectives of another person. It is a fundamental aspect of emotional intelligence and a key component of healthy social relationships. Empathy helps individuals connect with others, build trust, and respond compassionately to their needs and emotions.

Here are some ways to practice empathy:

1. Active Listening:

Pay full attention when someone is speaking to you.

Show that you are engaged by making eye contact, nodding, and providing verbal cues like "I see" or "I understand."

Avoid interrupting or formulating your response while the other person is talking.

2. Put Yourself in Their Shoes:

Try to imagine how the other person might be feeling. Consider their perspective, experiences, and emotions.

Reflect on how you would feel if you were in their situation.

3. Ask Open-ended Questions:

Encourage the person to share their thoughts and emotions by asking open-ended questions.

Open-ended questions begin with words like "how," "what," "tell me about," allowing the person to express themselves freely.

4. Practice Non-Verbal Communication:

Pay attention to non-verbal cues such as facial expressions, body language, and tone of voice.

Non-verbal cues often convey emotions more strongly than words alone.

5. Validate Their Feelings:

Acknowledge the other person's emotions without judgment. You can say things like "It's understandable that you feel that way" or "I can see why you might be upset."

Avoid dismissing or trivializing their feelings.

6. Cultivate Curiosity and Interest:

Be genuinely curious about the other person's experiences and feelings.

Ask follow-up questions to explore their emotions further.

7. Practice Mindfulness:

Be fully present in the moment and focus your attention on the other person.

Avoid distractions and be mindful of your own judgments and biases.

8. Show Compassion and Kindness:

Respond with kindness and compassion, even if you do not fully understand the other person's emotions.

Offer support and reassurance.

9. Reflect and Learn: After the interaction, reflect on what you have learned about the other person's experiences. Consider how this newfound understanding can inform your future interactions and relationships.

Empathy is a skill that can be developed and strengthened through practice and conscious effort. By actively practicing empathy, you can foster meaningful connections, improve communication, and contribute to a more compassionate and understanding world.

Empowering Stress-Free Living

The conclusion emphasizes the transformative potential of these stress management techniques. It reinforces that stress, while inevitable, can be effectively managed through emotional regulation and mindfulness. You are encouraged to incorporate these practices into your daily lives, knowing that by developing emotional resilience, you can face life's challenges with calmness, clarity, and a sense of inner peace.

3.3 CULTIVATING RESILIENCE: BUILDING EMOTIONAL RESILIENCE TO NAVIGATE LIFE'S CHALLENGES WITH GRACE AND BOUNCE BACK FROM SETBACKS.

"Our greatest glory is not in never falling, but in rising every time we fall." - Confucius

In this section, you will explore the concept of resilience as the ability to adapt and bounce back from life's challenges. The discussion focuses on the psychological aspects of resilience, emphasizing the importance of emotional regulation and positive thinking. The section introduces the "Resilience Inventory," a self-assessment exercise where you will reflect on past challenges and identify the strengths and coping strategies you used. This practice initiates the journey toward building emotional resilience.

Emotional Regulation and Resilience

This section delves into the relationship between emotional regulation and resilience. You will learn about the impact of managing emotions effectively on building resilience. The section introduces the "Emotion Release Technique," where you will visualize releasing negative emotions as they breathe out, creating space for positivity and resilience. This exercise empowers you to recognize the power of letting go and embracing emotional balance in building resilience.

Cultivating a Growth Mindset

The focus shifts to fostering a growth mindset, a key component of resilience. The section explores how embracing challenges and learning from failures contribute to resilience. You will engage in the "Failure to Growth Reflection," where they journal about a past failure, analyzing the lessons learned and the personal growth that ensued. By reframing failures as opportunities for growth, readers enhance your resilience mindset.

Failure to Growth Reflection, also known as "failure to growth mindset," refers to the concept of transforming setbacks, mistakes, and failures into opportunities for learning, personal development, and growth. It involves adopting a mindset that views failure not as a permanent indication of one's abilities or worth but as a steppingstone toward improvement and success.

Here is how the process of failure to growth reflection works:

Acknowledge the Failure: The first step is to acknowledge the failure or setback without denial or avoidance. It is essential to confront the situation honestly and recognize what went wrong.

Accept Responsibility: Take responsibility for your actions and decisions without self-blame or excessive guilt. Accept that mistakes happen, and that failure is a natural part of the learning process.

Reflect on the Experience: Reflect on the failure with a growth-oriented perspective. Ask yourself questions like:

What can I learn from this experience?

What specific factors contributed to the failure?

How can I improve or approach the situation differently next time?

Are there skills or knowledge areas I need to develop?

Identify Lessons Learned: Focus on the lessons learned from the failure. Consider the skills, knowledge, or strategies you gained insight into. These lessons can be valuable assets for future endeavors.

Embrace a Growth Mindset: Cultivate a growth mindset, which is the belief that abilities and intelligence can be developed with effort, dedication, and learning. Embrace challenges as opportunities to learn and improve, rather than threats to your self-worth.

Set New Goals: Based on the lessons learned, set new goals and action plans. Identify specific steps you can take to enhance your skills, knowledge, or approach to similar situations in the future.

Practice Self-Compassion: Be kind and compassionate toward yourself. Understand that everyone makes mistakes and encounters failures. Treat yourself with the same kindness you would offer to a friend facing a similar situation.

Seek Support: Talk to supportive friends, family, mentors, or colleagues about your experience. Sharing your thoughts and feelings can provide valuable perspectives and emotional support.

By embracing failure as an opportunity for growth and reflecting on the experience with a growth mindset, individuals can transform setbacks into valuable learning experiences. This mindset shift not only fosters resilience but also encourages continuous self-improvement and personal development.

Building Social Support Networks

This section discusses the role of social connections in resilience. You will learn about the importance of seeking support from friends, family, and community. The section introduces the "Gratitude for Support Exercise," where you will express gratitude to people who have supported you during challenging times. This practice reinforces the value of social connections, enhancing resilience through a sense of belonging and support.

Gratitude for Support Exercise is a mindfulness practice that involves expressing thankfulness for the support you receive from others. It is a simple yet powerful technique to enhance positive emotions, improve relationships, and foster a sense of well-being. Here is how you can practice the gratitude for support exercise:

1. Reflect on Supportive People: Take a moment to think about the people in your life who have offered you support, encouragement, or assistance. These could be friends, family members, colleagues, mentors, or anyone who has been there for you in times of need.

2. Identify Specific Acts of Support: Reflect on specific instances where these individuals supported you. It could be emotional support during a difficult time, practical help with a task, or even a kind word that lifted your spirits. Be as specific as possible.

3. Acknowledge the Impact: Consider how their support made a difference in your life. Reflect on the positive outcomes, your emotional well-being, or any challenges you were able to overcome due to their assistance.

4. Express Gratitude: Take a moment to express your gratitude. This can be done internally through mindful reflection or, if appropriate, you can express your gratitude directly to the person. You can write a thank-you note, make a phone call, or even express your thanks in person.

5. Feel the Gratitude: As you express your gratitude, try to connect with the positive emotions associated with the support you received. Feel the warmth, love, or relief that their support brought into your life.

6. Practice Regularly: Make this exercise a regular practice. You can do it daily, weekly, or as needed. The key is consistency. The more you practice gratitude for support, the more you will notice positive changes in your mindset and overall outlook.

Benefits of Gratitude for Support Exercise:

Enhanced Well-Being: Expressing gratitude has been linked to increased happiness and life satisfaction.

Improved Relationships: Gratitude strengthens social bonds and encourages reciprocity in relationships.

Reduced Stress: Focusing on positive aspects and support can help reduce stress and anxiety.

Positive Perspective: Gratitude shifts your focus from what is lacking to what you have, fostering a more positive outlook on life.

Practicing gratitude for support not only benefits you but also strengthens your relationships, creating a positive cycle of support and appreciation in your social network.

Mindfulness and Resilience

The last section explores mindfulness as a tool for building resilience. The section introduces the "Mindful Reflection Practice," where you will reflect on a challenging situation mindfully, observing your thoughts and emotions without judgment. Through this exercise, you will develop self-awareness and emotional regulation, crucial skills for resilience. Additionally, you will learn about the practice of mindfulness meditation and its role in cultivating resilience by promoting mental clarity and calmness.

Mindful reflection practice involves the intentional and non-judgmental contemplation of one's thoughts, emotions, and experiences in the present moment. It combines the principles of mindfulness and reflection, encouraging individuals to observe their thoughts and feelings without judgment, allowing for a deeper understanding of themselves and their experiences. Here is how you can practice mindful reflection:

1. Find a Quiet Space: Choose a quiet and comfortable place where you will not be disturbed. Sit or lie down in a relaxed but alert posture.

2. Focus on Your Breath: Start by bringing your attention to your breath. Notice the sensation of the breath entering and leaving your body. Use your breath as an anchor to keep you grounded in the present moment.

3. Acknowledge Your Thoughts: Allow your thoughts to arise naturally. You do not need to force or suppress any thoughts. Acknowledge whatever thoughts come to mind without judgment. Imagine them as clouds passing by in the sky.

4. Observe Your Emotions: Notice any emotions that arise within you. Whether it is happiness, sadness, frustration, or calmness, observe these emotions without getting carried away by them. Allow them to be present

without attachment or resistance.

5. Be Aware of Sensations: Pay attention to any physical sensations in your body. It could be warmth, tension, relaxation, or any other feelings. Scan your body from head to toe, noting any sensations without judgment.

6. Practice Non-Judgmental Awareness: If judgmental thoughts arise (e.g., "I shouldn't be feeling this way" or "This thought is wrong"), acknowledge these judgments without judgment. Be compassionate with yourself and gently guide your focus back to observing your thoughts and feelings.

7. Cultivate a Curious Attitude: Approach your thoughts and emotions with curiosity. Ask yourself why you might be feeling a certain way or what might be the root cause of a particular thought. Be open to exploring your inner experiences.

8. Reflect Silently: After observing your thoughts, emotions, and sensations, you can silently reflect on your experiences. Ask yourself questions like, "What did I learn about myself?" or "How can I respond skillfully to these thoughts and emotions in the future?"

9. Conclude Mindfully: When you are ready to conclude your practice, take a few deep breaths and gradually bring your awareness back to your surroundings. Carry the sense of mindfulness and self-awareness with you as you continue your day.

Mindful reflection practice helps individuals develop self-awareness, emotional regulation, and a deeper understanding of their thought patterns and emotions. Regular practice can lead to greater insight, improved well-being, and enhanced overall mindfulness in daily life.

The Resilient Path Forward

The conclusion emphasizes the transformative journey you have undertaken in cultivating resilience. It reinforces that resilience is not just a trait but a skill that can be developed through practice and mindset shifts. You are encouraged to continue incorporating emotional regulation, positive thinking, social connections, and mindfulness into your life, knowing that by doing so, you can navigate life's challenges with grace, bounce back from setbacks, and lead a more resilient and empowered life.

3.4 EMOTIONAL FREEDOM: TECHNIQUES TO RELEASE NEGATIVE EMOTIONS AND CULTIVATE A SENSE OF EMOTIONAL FREEDOM AND BALANCE.

"The only way to deal with fear is to face it head on." - James Dyson

In this section, you will explore the concept of emotional freedom as the ability to release negative emotions and experience inner balance. The discussion focuses on the psychological and physiological impact of unresolved emotions. The section introduces the "Emotional Release Journal," encouraging you to write about your negative emotions and the situations triggering them. This practice initiates the process of acknowledging and understanding these emotions, essential steps toward emotional freedom.

Emotional Awareness and Acceptance

This section delves into the importance of emotional awareness and acceptance in achieving emotional freedom. You will learn about the power of acknowledging and accepting all emotions without judgment. The section introduces the "Body Scan Meditation," where readers systematically focus on various parts of their body, paying attention to any emotions or tensions. This practice promotes self-awareness and acceptance, laying the foundation for emotional freedom.

Techniques for Emotional Release

The focus shifts to practical techniques for releasing negative emotions. The section explores exercises such as journaling, creative expression, and physical activities. You will engage in the "Creative Expression Therapy," where you will use art, writing, or music to express your emotions freely. By externalizing your emotions, you will experience a sense of relief, paving the way for emotional freedom and inner balance.

Creative expression therapy, also known as expressive arts therapy or creative arts therapy, is a therapeutic approach that uses various forms of creative expression to help individuals explore their emotions, improve mental well-being, and promote personal growth. It encompasses a wide range of artistic activities such as painting, drawing, writing, music, dance, drama, and other forms of creative expression. The focus is not on the artistic quality of the work but on the process of creation and the emotions and insights it generates.

Here are key aspects of creative expression therapy:

1. Non-Verbal Communication: Creative expression provides a non-verbal means of communication. For individuals who find it difficult to express their feelings and thoughts verbally, engaging in artistic activities can serve as a powerful outlet.

2. Emotional Release: Through creative expression, individuals can release pent-up emotions, trauma, or stress in a safe and supportive environment. Art, music, movement, and other forms of expression can act as a channel for emotions that are difficult to articulate verbally.

3. Self-Exploration: Engaging in creative activities encourages self-exploration and self-discovery. It allows

individuals to explore their subconscious mind, uncover hidden emotions, and gain insights into their personal experiences.

4. Empowerment: Creative expression therapy empowers individuals by giving them a sense of control over their artistic choices. This empowerment can translate into increased confidence and self-esteem in other areas of life.

5. Therapeutic Relationship: The therapeutic relationship between the client and the therapist is crucial in creative expression therapy. The therapist provides a safe and non-judgmental space, offering guidance and support while encouraging the individual's creative process.

6. Integration of Mind and Body: Creative expression therapy integrates the mind and body, allowing individuals to connect with their emotions on a visceral level. This mind-body connection can facilitate emotional healing and overall well-being.

7. Holistic Approach: Creative expression therapy takes a holistic approach to healing, considering the individual's emotional, mental, physical, and spiritual aspects. It addresses the whole person rather than focusing solely on symptoms or problems.

8. Flexibility and Adaptability: Creative expression therapy can be adapted to various populations and age groups, making it suitable for children, adolescents, adults, and seniors. It is used in diverse settings, including mental health clinics, schools, hospitals, and community centers.

Creative expression therapy is conducted by licensed therapists trained in both traditional therapeutic techniques and creative arts modalities. It can be a valuable adjunct to traditional talk therapy, providing individuals with additional avenues for self-expression and personal growth.

Forgiveness and Letting Go

This section discusses the transformative power of forgiveness in achieving emotional freedom. You will learn about the connection between forgiveness, releasing grudges, and emotional well-being. The section introduces the "Forgiveness Letter Writing Exercise," guiding you to write a letter to someone they need to forgive, expressing their feelings and granting forgiveness. This practice promotes emotional closure, enabling you to let go of the past and experience emotional freedom.

Forgiveness letter writing exercise is a therapeutic technique where an individual writes a letter to someone who has hurt or wronged them in the past. The purpose of this exercise is to facilitate the process of forgiveness, which can be deeply healing and transformative. The letter allows individuals to express their feelings, release negative emotions, and ultimately, work towards letting go of resentment and finding peace.

Here is how you can approach the forgiveness letter writing exercise:

1. Choose the Recipient: Select the person you want to forgive. This could be someone from your past, a family member, a friend, a romantic partner, or even yourself. The person chosen should be someone you have unresolved negative feelings towards.

2. Set the Tone: Begin the letter in a calm and composed manner. Acknowledge the person by name and state that you are writing the letter to address your feelings and work towards forgiveness.

3. Express Your Feelings: Be honest about how their actions made you feel. Describe the pain, anger, or sadness

you experienced as a result of their behavior. It is important to express your emotions openly, allowing yourself to confront the impact of their actions on your life.

4. Acknowledge Their Perspective: Try to see the situation from their point of view. This does not mean justifying their actions but understanding that people make mistakes or behave hurtfully due to their own struggles, insecurities, or challenges.

5. State Your Decision to Forgive: Clearly state that you are choosing to forgive them. This decision is not about condoning their actions but about releasing the burden of resentment from your own heart. State your intention to move forward without carrying the weight of anger or grudges.

6. Express Empathy: Express empathy towards the person. Acknowledge their humanity and the possibility of them making amends or changing in the future. This can create a sense of understanding and closure.

7. End on a Positive Note: End the letter on a positive and hopeful note. Wish them well in their life and genuinely hope that they find happiness and peace. This signifies your willingness to let go of negativity and move forward.

8. Reflect and Release: After writing the letter, take some time to reflect on your feelings. You can choose to keep the letter as a personal exercise or, if you feel comfortable, you might decide to send it. Sending the letter is optional and depends on your individual circumstances.

The forgiveness letter writing exercise can be a deeply emotional and cathartic experience. It allows individuals to confront their pain, process their feelings, and ultimately, make the choice to free themselves from the emotional burden of past grievances.

Cultivating Emotional Balance Through Mindfulness

The last section explores mindfulness as a tool for cultivating emotional balance and freedom. The section introduces the "Mindful Emotional Observation," where you will observe your emotions without attachment, allowing them to rise and fade naturally. By practicing non-judgmental awareness, you will learn to detach from your emotions, achieving a sense of emotional freedom and inner peace.

Embracing Emotional Liberation

The conclusion emphasizes the transformative journey you have undertaken in achieving emotional freedom. It reinforces that emotional freedom is not about eliminating negative emotions but about accepting, understanding, and releasing them in a healthy way. You are encouraged to continue practicing emotional awareness, acceptance, and forgiveness, integrating these techniques into their lives. By doing so, you can achieve emotional liberation, leading a more balanced, harmonious, and emotionally free life.

3.5 MINDFULNESS AND EMOTIONAL REGULATION: EXPLORING THE CONNECTION BETWEEN MINDFULNESS PRACTICES AND EMOTIONAL REGULATION FOR A MORE CENTERED AND PEACEFUL LIFE.

"Between stimulus and response, there is a space. In that space is our power to choose our response. In our response lies our growth and our freedom." - Viktor Frankl

In this section, you will delve into the foundational concepts of mindfulness and emotional regulation. The discussion focuses on the interplay between mindfulness practices and the ability to manage emotions effectively. The section introduces the "Mindful Breathing Exercise," guiding you to focus on their breath, enhancing awareness of the present moment. This practice sets the stage for understanding the connection between mindful awareness and emotional regulation.

Mindfulness Meditation for Emotional Clarity

This section explores mindfulness meditation as a tool for achieving emotional clarity. You will learn about the practice of mindful meditation and its impact on emotional awareness. The section introduces the "Body Scan Meditation," guiding you to scan their body, noting any areas of tension or discomfort. Through this practice, readers enhance their emotional awareness, gaining insights into how emotions manifest physically, paving the way for emotional regulation.

Mindfulness-Based Stress Reduction (MBSR) Techniques

The focus shifts to Mindfulness-Based Stress Reduction (MBSR) techniques. The section discusses how MBSR practices enhance emotional regulation by reducing stress. You will engage in the "Mindful Walking Exercise," encouraging them to walk mindfully, focusing on each step and the sensations in their body. By practicing mindful movement, readers learn to regulate their emotions, even in the midst of daily activities.

Mindful walking, also known as walking meditation, is a form of meditation that involves walking slowly and deliberately while maintaining a heightened awareness of your body and surroundings. Unlike traditional meditation where you sit in one place, mindful walking incorporates movement, making it an excellent practice for those who find stillness challenging or prefer an active form of meditation. Here is how you can practice mindful walking:

1. Find a Quiet Space: Choose a quiet and peaceful place to walk. It could be a garden, a park, a quiet street, or any location where you can walk without distractions.

2. Begin with Stillness: Stand still for a moment, grounding yourself. Feel the connection between your feet and the ground. Take a few deep breaths to center yourself.

3. Start Walking Slowly: Start walking at a slower pace than usual. Pay attention to each step you take. Notice the lifting, moving, and placing down of your feet. Feel the subtle movements and sensations in your legs and feet.

4. Focus on Your Breath: As you walk, synchronize your breath with your steps. For example, you can take one breath for every two or three steps. Focus on the sensation of your breath entering and leaving your body.

5. Be Present: Engage your senses. Notice the sights, sounds, and smells around you. Feel the breeze on your skin, listen to the chirping of birds, or notice the rustling of leaves. Be fully present in the moment.

6. Mindful Awareness: If your mind starts to wander, gently bring your focus back to your breath and your steps. Be aware of any thoughts, emotions, or sensations that arise without judgment. Acknowledge them and let them pass, returning your attention to your walking.

7. Walking Gratitude: Optionally, you can practice gratitude during mindful walking. With each step, think of something you are grateful for. It could be a person, a situation, or even the ability to walk. Feel the gratitude in your heart as you continue walking.

8. End Mindfully: When you decide to conclude your mindful walk, gradually slow down your pace. Stand still again for a moment, appreciating the experience. Notice how you feel after the practice.

Mindful walking can be practiced for short or extended periods. It encourages a sense of calm, presence, and awareness. Regular practice can enhance your mindfulness skills, reduce stress, and improve your overall well-being. Remember, the key is to walk with intention, awareness, and a sense of appreciation for the simple act of walking.

Mindfulness and Emotion Acceptance

This section explores the role of mindfulness in accepting and embracing all emotions, including challenging ones. The section introduces the "R.A.I.N. Meditation" (Recognize, Accept, Investigate, Non-Identification), guiding readers through a structured meditation to navigate difficult emotions. By accepting emotions without judgment, readers cultivate emotional regulation through mindfulness, allowing emotions to arise and dissipate naturally.

RAIN is a mindfulness and self-compassion meditation practice developed by Tara Brach, a renowned meditation teacher and psychologist. The RAIN meditation technique is a simple yet powerful method for dealing with difficult emotions, challenging situations, or moments of self-criticism. The acronym RAIN stands for Recognize, Allow, Investigate, and Nurture, and it guides you through a process of self-reflection and emotional healing. Here is how you can practice RAIN meditation:

**1. Recognize: Begin by recognizing and acknowledging the emotion or thought that you are experiencing. It might be fear, anger, sadness, self-doubt, or any other challenging feeling. Instead of ignoring or suppressing it, simply acknowledge its presence.

**2. Allow: Allow the emotion to be there without judgment. Accept it as a natural part of being human. Often, our suffering intensifies when we resist or fight against our emotions. Instead, give yourself permission to feel what you are feeling.

**3. Investigate: Investigate the emotion with gentle curiosity. Ask yourself questions like:

What does this feeling remind me of?

Where do I feel it in my body?

What thoughts are associated with this emotion?

Is there a story or belief connected to this feeling?

Explore the emotion without getting lost in the story or narrative. Observe it as if you are studying it objectively.

**4. Nurture: Finally, nurture yourself with self-compassion and kindness. Offer yourself the same care and understanding that you would give to a dear friend in a similar situation. This might involve offering words of comfort, placing a hand on your heart, or simply sending feelings of warmth and kindness to yourself.

Tips for RAIN Meditation:

Practice Regularly: You can use the RAIN meditation technique whenever you encounter challenging emotions or situations. It is a portable practice that you can do anywhere, anytime.

Be Patient: It might take time to fully embrace this practice, especially if you are accustomed to being self-critical. Be patient with yourself and approach the process with gentleness.

Cultivate Self-Compassion: The nurturing step (Nurture) is a vital aspect of RAIN meditation. Treat yourself with the same kindness and compassion you would offer to a close friend.

RAIN meditation is a transformative practice that helps individuals build emotional resilience, self-compassion, and self-awareness. It empowers you to face difficult emotions with mindfulness and understanding, fostering emotional healing and well-being

Cultivating Mindful Responses to Emotions

The last section focuses on integrating mindfulness into daily responses to emotions. The section discusses how mindful responses, such as compassionate self-talk and non-reactive observation, enhance emotional regulation. You will practice the "Mindful Response Journaling," where they journal about a triggering situation, exploring their thoughts and emotions with mindful awareness. Through this practice, readers learn to respond consciously, rather than react impulsively, fostering emotional regulation and inner peace.

The Harmony of Mindfulness and Emotional Regulation

The conclusion emphasizes the transformative constructive interaction between mindfulness and emotional regulation. It reinforces that mindfulness practices offer a path to emotional balance, enabling readers to respond to life's challenges with centeredness and calm. You are encouraged to continue their mindfulness journey, integrating these practices into their lives, knowing that through the harmonious integration of mindfulness and emotional regulation, they can lead a more centered, peaceful, and emotionally balanced life.

CHAPTER FIVE

EMPATHY AND SOCIAL SKILLS

"Treat others how you want to be treated." - Ancient Golden Rule

In my journey of developing empathy and social skills, I encountered a shy classmate named Ashok. Despite his reserved nature, I sensed his struggle to fit in. Taking a step back, I put myself in his shoes, imagining the challenges he faced. Empathy guided my actions; I approached him with genuine kindness, inviting him into our circle. Over time, my understanding and patience encouraged him to open up. Our friendship blossomed, and I witnessed the power of empathy in bridging social gaps. This experience taught me that embracing empathy and honing social skills not only enriches others' lives but also fosters genuine connections and understanding.

In today's fast-paced world, empathy and social skills play a crucial role in fostering meaningful connections and building strong relationships. With the rise of emotional intelligence, individuals are now recognizing the significance of empathy in navigating diverse social contexts. In this section, we will explore the various aspects of empathy, its connection to social skills, and the impact of emotional intelligence in enhancing these abilities.

Understanding Empathy

Empathy, often referred to as the ability to understand and share the feelings of others, forms the foundation of effective social interactions. By putting ourselves in someone else's shoes, we gain insight into their experiences, emotions, and perspectives. Empathy involves both cognitive and emotional components, allowing us to not only comprehend others' feelings but also respond to them with sensitivity and compassion.

Figure:14

Empathy and Social Skills

Empathy and social skills go hand in hand, as one's ability to understand and connect with others directly impacts their social interactions. When individuals possess an elevated level of empathy, they become adept at recognizing non-verbal cues, understanding social dynamics, and adapting their behavior accordingly.

Empathetic individuals are more likely to engage in active listening, effective communication, and conflict resolution, leading to stronger and more harmonious relationships.

The Role of Emotional Intelligence

Emotional intelligence, often abbreviated as EQ, encompasses a range of skills that contribute to emotional awareness, self-management, and effective interpersonal relationships. Empathy forms a crucial component of emotional intelligence, as it involves recognizing and regulating our own emotions while also understanding and responding to the emotions of others. By developing emotional intelligence, individuals can cultivate empathy and harness its power to navigate social situations with finesse.

Cultivating Empathy and Social Skills

Empathy and social skills are not fixed traits but can be developed and strengthened over time. One way to cultivate empathy is by actively practicing perspective-taking exercises, such as imagining oneself in different scenarios or engaging in role-playing activities. Additionally, fostering self-awareness and emotional regulation through mindfulness and reflection can enhance both empathy and social skills. Seeking opportunities for meaningful social interactions, volunteering, and engaging in active listening are also effective ways to hone these abilities.

In a world that thrives on connections, empathy and social skills are invaluable assets. By embracing empathy and harnessing the power of emotional intelligence, individuals can forge deeper connections, foster understanding, and contribute to a more compassionate society. As we continue to prioritize empathy and social skills, we pave the way for a more empathetic and harmonious world.

4.1 THE POWER OF EMPATHY: UNDERSTANDING THE ROLE OF EMPATHY IN BUILDING MEANINGFUL RELATIONSHIPS AND FOSTERING CONNECTION.

"Wisdom is the reward you get for a lifetime of listening when you'd have preferred to talk." - Doug Larson

In this section, you will explore the fundamental concept of empathy and its significance in human connections. The discussion emphasizes the empathetic understanding of emotions, thoughts, and experiences of others. The section introduces the "Empathy Walk," encouraging readers to consciously observe people around them, imagining their experiences and emotions. This practice initiates the journey toward understanding the world from others' perspectives, a key element of empathy.

Figure:15

Empathy in Communication

This section delves into the role of empathy in effective communication. You will learn about active listening, non-verbal cues, and empathetic responses. The section introduces the "Reflective Listening Exercise," where readers practice mirroring the emotions and statements of the speaker. Through this exercise, readers enhance their empathetic communication skills, fostering deeper connections with others.

Empathy in Relationships

The focus shifts to empathy's transformative impact on relationships. The section discusses empathetic understanding, emotional validation, and supporting loved ones. You will engage in the "Empathy Journaling," where they write about a recent interaction where they felt deeply understood or misunderstood. This reflective practice deepens self-awareness and enhances empathy in relationships, fostering emotional intimacy.

Figure:16

Empathy in Conflict Resolution

This section explores empathy as a tool for resolving conflicts peacefully. You will learn about empathetic negotiation, understanding diverse perspectives, and finding common ground. The section introduces the "Empathetic Role Reversal," where readers mentally switch places with the person they conflict with, understanding the situation from their viewpoint. This exercise promotes empathy and compassion, facilitating constructive conflict resolution.

Cultivating Self-Empathy and Compassion

The last section focuses on self-empathy and self-compassion as foundations for empathetic connections with others. The section discusses self-awareness, self-acceptance, and self-kindness. You will practice "Loving-Kindness Meditation," where they extend feelings of love and compassion to themselves and others. Through this practice, readers nurture a positive relationship with themselves, enhancing their capacity for empathetic connections with the world.

The Transformative Power of Empathy

The conclusion emphasizes the profound impact of empathy on personal relationships, societal harmony, and emotional well-being. It reinforces that empathy is a skill that can be cultivated, leading to more compassionate and interconnected communities. You are encouraged to continue practicing empathy, knowing that through their empathetic connections, they contribute to a kinder, more understanding, and empathetic world.

Tips:Practice active listening and empathetic understanding. Cultivating genuine curiosity about others' perspectives and emotions strengthens empathy and social skills, enriching your relationships and fostering a compassionate community

4.2 ACTIVE LISTENING: DEVELOPING ACTIVE LISTENING SKILLS TO ENHANCE EMPATHY AND CREATE DEEPER CONNECTIONS WITH OTHERS.

"Most people do not listen with the intent to understand; they listen with the intent to reply." - Stephen R. Covey

In this section, you will explore the essence of active listening as the foundation for meaningful connections. The discussion emphasizes the importance of being present, fully engaged, and empathetically attuned to others. The section introduces the "Silent Mindfulness Listening Exercise," encouraging readers to practice silence while someone speaks, focusing entirely on the speaker without formulating responses. This practice initiates the journey toward developing genuine active listening skills.

Figure:17

Empathy and Active Listening

This section delves into the profound connection between empathy and active listening. You will learn how active listening enhances empathetic understanding and fosters deeper connections. The section introduces the "Reflective Empathy Exercise," where readers mirror the emotions and experiences shared by the speaker. Through this practice, readers not only develop their active listening skills but also cultivate genuine empathy.

Non-Verbal Communication and Active Listening

The focus shifts to non-verbal cues and their role in active listening. The section discusses body language, eye contact, and facial expressions. You will engage in the "Non-Verbal Awareness Activity," where they observe and interpret non-verbal cues in a conversation without words. This exercise heightens sensitivity to unspoken communication, enhancing active listening skills and empathetic connections.

Overcoming Barriers to Active Listening

This section explores common barriers to active listening, such as distractions and preconceived notions. You will learn strategies to overcome these barriers and enhance their listening skills. The section introduces the "Focused Attention Exercise," where readers practice listening to a specific sound or voice amidst background noise, sharpening their focus and concentration. Through this exercise, readers develop resilience against distractions, strengthening their active listening abilities.

Cultivating Mindful Listening in Daily Interactions

The last section focuses on integrating active listening into daily interactions through mindfulness. The section discusses the role of mindfulness in staying present and attentive. You will practice "Mindful Listening Meditation," where they listen to various sounds mindfully, appreciating the richness of each sound. By extending this mindfulness to conversations, readers enhance their active listening skills, creating deeper connections with others.

The Power of Listening

The conclusion emphasizes the transformative potential of active listening in building genuine connections, resolving conflicts, and fostering empathy. It reinforces that active listening is not just a communication skill but a way of being present and utterly understanding others. You are encouraged to continue practicing active listening, knowing that through their attentive and empathetic presence, they can create a more compassionate, understanding, and harmonious world.

4.3 NON-VERBAL COMMUNICATION: EXPLORING THE IMPORTANCE OF NON-VERBAL CUES IN UNDERSTANDING AND EXPRESSING EMOTIONS EFFECTIVELY.

"Empathy is about finding echoes of another person in yourself."-Mohsin Hamid

In this section, you will delve into the world of non-verbal communication and its significance in human interactions. The discussion focuses on the power of gestures, facial expressions, posture, and eye contact. The section introduces the "Non-Verbal Observation Exercise," encouraging readers to observe people in various situations and interpret their emotions and intentions solely based on non-verbal cues. This practice initiates the journey toward understanding the unspoken language of emotions.

Reading Facial Expressions and Emotions

This section explores the intricate language of facial expressions and how they convey emotions. You will learn about micro expressions, subtle facial movements that reveal hidden emotions. The section introduces the "Emotion Recognition Game," where readers identify emotions from facial expressions in pictures. By honing their facial expression recognition skills, readers enhance their emotional intelligence and empathy.

Body Language and Posture

The focus shifts to body language and posture as powerful indicators of emotions and intentions. The section discusses open and closed body language, as well as power poses. You will engage in the "Body Language Awareness Practice," where they consciously adjust their posture and observe the impact on their emotions. This exercise enhances self-awareness and sensitivity to the body language of others, facilitating more effective and empathetic communication.

The Role of Voice and Tone

This section delves into the nuances of voice modulation, tone, pitch, and volume in communication. You will learn how vocal cues convey emotions and attitudes. The section introduces the "Voice Modulation Exercise," where readers practice conveying different emotions through variations in their tone and pitch. By mastering vocal nuances, readers enhance their ability to express emotions effectively and understand the emotions of others.

Non-Verbal Communication in Different Cultures

The last section focuses on cultural differences in non-verbal communication. The section discusses how gestures and expressions vary across cultures and the importance of cultural sensitivity. You will practice the "Cross-Cultural Non-Verbal Exchange," where they explore non-verbal gestures from diverse cultures and their meanings.

Through this exercise, readers develop cultural awareness, fostering respectful and empathetic communication in diverse settings.

Mastering the Art of Non-Verbal Communication

The conclusion emphasizes the transformative impact of mastering non-verbal communication skills. It reinforces that understanding and expressing emotions effectively through non-verbal cues enriches personal and professional relationships. You are encouraged to continue practicing non-verbal communication awareness, knowing that by honing these skills, they can navigate the complex realm of human emotions with sensitivity, empathy, and profound understanding.

4.4 BUILDING SOCIAL CONNECTIONS: STRATEGIES FOR CULTIVATING STRONG SOCIAL CONNECTIONS BOTH PERSONALLY AND PROFESSIONALLY.

"Empathy is the understanding that there are feelings and concerns beyond one's own and that the more one can identify with the feelings, needs, and concerns of others, the more effective a communicator one will be." - Virgil A. Kraft

In this section, you will explore the profound impact of social connections on mental, emotional, and physical well-being. The discussion emphasizes the importance of both personal and professional social networks. The section introduces the "Social Connection Reflection," encouraging readers to contemplate meaningful social connections in their lives and their positive effects. This practice initiates the journey toward understanding the significance of social bonds for overall happiness and fulfillment.

Effective Communication in Social Settings

This section delves into the art of effective communication as a foundation for building strong social connections. You will learn about active listening, empathetic responses, and assertive communication. The section introduces the "Active Listening Circle," where readers engage in a conversation, taking turns to actively listen and respond empathetically. Through this exercise, readers practice essential communication skills, fostering deeper connections in social interactions.

Nurturing Personal Relationships

The focus shifts to nurturing personal relationships, including friendships, family, and romantic partnerships. The section discusses qualities like trust, empathy, and emotional support. You will engage in the "Gratitude Jar Practice," where they write notes expressing gratitude for their loved ones and place them in a jar. This practice enhances appreciation for personal connections, strengthening the emotional bonds with family and friends.

Building Professional Networks

This section explores the significance of professional networks in career growth and personal development. You will learn networking strategies, effective communication in professional settings, and the art of mentorship. The section introduces the "Networking Elevator Pitch," guiding you to craft a concise introduction for professional gatherings. Through this exercise, readers refine their networking skills, establishing meaningful connections in their professional lives.

Cultivating Empathy and Emotional Intelligence

The last section focuses on empathy and emotional intelligence as cornerstones for building strong social connections. The section discusses understanding others' emotions, managing conflicts, and building a supportive social environment. You will practice the "Empathy Circle," where they share individual experiences and empathetically respond to others' stories. Through this practice, readers deepen their empathetic understanding, fostering a compassionate and supportive social community.

The Art of Building Lasting Connections

The conclusion emphasizes the transformative potential of building social connections both personally and professionally. It reinforces that genuine connections require empathy, active listening, and mutual respect. You are encouraged to continue practicing these skills, knowing that by nurturing social bonds, they enrich their lives with meaningful relationships, emotional support, and a sense of belonging. Building lasting connections is not just a social skill; it is a lifelong practice that leads to a more fulfilling and interconnected existence.

4.5 EMPATHY IN CONFLICT RESOLUTION: APPLYING EMPATHY AS A TOOL FOR RESOLVING CONFLICTS AND PROMOTING UNDERSTANDING IN RELATIONSHIPS.

"An eye for an eye only ends up making the whole world blind." - Mahatma Gandhi

Conflict is an inevitable part of human relationships. Whether it is a disagreement with a loved one, a clash at work, or a difference of opinion with a friend, conflicts can arise in various aspects of our lives. In such situations, empathy serves as a powerful tool for resolving conflicts and fostering understanding. By putting ourselves in the shoes of others and genuinely seeking to understand their perspectives and emotions, we can bridge the gap, find common ground, and navigate conflicts more effectively.

Defining Empathy in Conflict Resolution

Empathy is the ability to understand and share the feelings of another person. In conflict resolution, empathy involves actively listening to the other party, acknowledging their emotions, and demonstrating a genuine desire to understand their experiences. It goes beyond sympathy or agreement; empathy requires us to step outside of our own viewpoints and truly connect with the emotions and needs of others involved in the conflict.

The Role of Empathy in Resolving Conflicts

Empathy plays a crucial role in conflict resolution by fostering open communication, reducing defensiveness, and promoting mutual respect. When we approach conflicts with empathy, we create a safe space where both parties feel heard and validated. This open dialogue allows for a deeper understanding of each other's perspectives and motivations, paving the way for finding mutually beneficial solutions.

Cultivating Empathy in Conflict Resolution

Cultivating empathy requires intentional effort and practice. It begins with active listening, where we give our full attention to the other person without interrupting or judging. We can also practice empathy by asking open-ended questions to encourage the other person to share their thoughts and feelings more deeply. Additionally, reflecting on our own emotions and biases enables us to approach conflicts with a more empathetic mindset.

Overcoming Challenges in Applying Empathy

Applying empathy in conflict resolution is not without challenges. It can be difficult to empathize with someone whose actions or beliefs we strongly disagree with. However, understanding that empathy does not mean agreement helps us separate our own perspectives from the emotions and experiences of others. It requires patience, self-awareness, and the willingness to step outside our comfort zones.

Building Trust and Connection

One of the key benefits of emotional intelligence in leadership is the ability to foster trust and connection. Leaders who exhibit empathy, actively listen, and demonstrate genuine care for their team members create an environment of psychological safety. This fosters trust, encourages open communication, and promotes collaboration among team members, leading to higher productivity and engagement.

Enhancing Decision-Making

Leaders with high emotional intelligence possess the ability to make sound and rational decisions even in high-pressure situations. They can recognize and manage their own emotions, preventing impulsive reactions that may lead to poor decision-making. By considering the emotional impact of their choices on others, emotionally intelligent leaders make decisions that align with the best interests of both the organization and its employees.

Resolving Conflicts Effectively

Conflict is inevitable in any workplace, but emotionally intelligent leaders have the skills to navigate and resolve conflicts in a constructive manner. By understanding the underlying emotions and perspectives of those involved, they can facilitate open dialogue, find common ground, and reach mutually beneficial resolutions. This not only resolves immediate conflicts but also strengthens relationships and builds a more harmonious work environment.

In conclusion, emotional intelligence is a powerful asset for leaders seeking to make a positive impact on their teams and organizations. By developing and honing their emotional intelligence skills, leaders can create a culture of trust, enhance decision-making processes, and effectively resolve conflicts. Incorporating emotional intelligence in leadership practices is a transformative approach that can unlock personal and professional growth, driving both individual and organizational success.

In conclusion, empathy is a powerful tool for resolving conflicts and promoting understanding in relationships. By actively listening, seeking to understand, and validating the emotions of others, we create an environment that fosters open communication and mutual respect. While empathy may not always result in immediate resolution, it sets the foundation for finding common ground and building stronger, more empathetic relationships.

CHAPTER SIX

EMOTIONAL INTELLIGENCE IN LEADERSHIP

"The best leaders are those most interested in surrounding themselves with assistants and associates smarter than they are." - John C. Maxwell

Nelson Mandela: As a prominent historical figure, Nelson Mandela showcased emotional intelligence throughout his leadership odyssey. Confronting immense challenges, he demonstrated exceptional empathy, grasping the challenges faced by others and using this understanding to create bonds and foster connections. Mandela's skill in managing his emotions allowed him to stay resolute in his quest for justice without giving in to bitterness or vengeance. His steadfast dedication to reconciliation not only influenced his nation but also left a profound impact on the entire globe.

In today's fast-paced and ever-changing business landscape, effective in this section, you will explore the fundamental role of empathy in resolving conflicts. The discussion emphasizes empathetic understanding, active listening, and perspective-taking. The section introduces the "Empathy Mapping Exercise," where readers visually map out their own and the other party's emotions, thoughts, and needs during a conflict situation. This practice initiates the journey toward understanding the conflict from multiple perspectives, a crucial step in empathetic conflict resolution.

Figure:18

Empathetic Communication Techniques

Mahatma Gandhi: Mahatma Gandhi's enduring impact as a transformative leader stems from his remarkable emotional intelligence. Demonstrating steadfast self-awareness and self-control, he embodied integrity and moral courage, becoming an inspiration for millions during India's fight for independence. Gandhi's empathetic demeanor allowed him to forge connections across diverse communities, fostering understanding with compassion and advocating peaceful resistance as a potent catalyst for transformation.

This section delves into empathetic communication techniques, including non-verbal cues, tone of voice, and validating emotions. You will learn about the importance of validating the emotions of others in conflict resolution. The section introduces the "Validation Circle," where participants validate each other's emotions and experiences during a simulated conflict scenario. This exercise enhances readers' ability to acknowledge others' feelings, fostering a more empathetic approach to conflict resolution.

Empathy and De-escalation Strategies

The focus shifts to de-escalation strategies rooted in empathy. The section discusses active listening, de-escalation language, and finding common ground. You will engage in the "Mirroring Technique," where they mirror the emotions and words of the conflicted party, creating a sense of connection and understanding. Through this practice, readers learn to de-escalate tense situations by empathetically reflecting the other party's emotions.

Empathy and Forgiveness

This section explores the connection between empathy and forgiveness in conflict resolution. You will learn how empathy fosters understanding, leading to genuine forgiveness and reconciliation. The section introduces the "Empathetic Forgiveness Letter," guiding you to write a letter from the perspective of the person they conflict with, expressing their feelings and seeking understanding. This practice encourages readers to empathize deeply, paving the way for forgiveness and healing.

Building Empathy Skills for Sustainable Relationships

The last section focuses on building empathy skills for long-term, sustainable relationships. The section discusses self-empathy, boundary setting, and empathy as a foundation for healthy relationships. You will practice the "Self-Compassion Meditation," where they extend empathy and understanding to themselves, embracing their imperfections. Through this exercise, readers cultivate self-empathy, enhancing their capacity for empathetic interactions and conflict resolution in all relationships.

Empathy as the Path to Lasting Peace

It emphasizes the transformative power of empathy in resolving conflicts and fostering understanding in relationships. It reinforces that empathetic conflict resolution is not just a skill but a mindset, rooted in genuine understanding and compassion. You are encouraged to continue practicing empathy, knowing that through their empathetic approach, they contribute to peaceful resolutions, strengthened relationships, and a more harmonious world. Empathy, when embraced wholeheartedly, becomes the bridge to lasting peace in all relationships. goes beyond mere technical skills and expertise. Emotional intelligence, often overlooked but incredibly crucial, plays a pivotal role in successful leadership. In this section, we will explore the significance of emotional intelligence in leadership and how it can transform the way we lead and inspire others.

5.1 THE ROLE OF EMOTIONAL INTELLIGENCE IN LEADERSHIP: EXPLORING HOW EMOTIONAL INTELLIGENCE INFLUENCES LEADERSHIP EFFECTIVENESS AND SUCCESS.

"A leader is one who knows the way, goes the way, and shows the way." - John C. Maxwell

In this section, you will explore the concept of emotional intelligence (EI) and its pivotal role in effective leadership. The discussion emphasizes self-awareness, self-regulation, empathy, and social skills as key components of EI. The section introduces the "Emotional Self-Assessment," guiding you to reflect on their emotional strengths and areas for growth. This practice initiates the journey toward understanding the importance of EI in leadership effectiveness.

EI and Self-Management in Leadership

This section delves into the significance of self-management in leadership, focusing on emotional regulation and resilience. You will learn strategies for managing stress, handling criticism, and maintaining composure under pressure. The section introduces the "Emotional Resilience Practice," where readers visualize challenging scenarios and practice responding with calm and poise. This exercise enhances self-management skills, crucial for effective leadership.

Empathy and Social Awareness in Leadership

The focus shifts to empathy and social awareness as essential skills for empathetic and socially intelligent leadership. The section discusses active listening, understanding diverse perspectives, and fostering a supportive organizational culture. You will engage in the "Empathy in Action Exercise," where they practice active listening and respond empathetically to colleagues' concerns. Through this practice, readers enhance their empathy and social awareness, vital for fostering positive relationships within the team.

EI and Relationship Management in Leadership

This section explores relationship management skills, including conflict resolution, effective communication, and building trust. You will learn techniques for resolving conflicts, providing constructive feedback, and fostering a collaborative environment. The section introduces the

"Trust-Building Workshop," where readers participate in team-building activities that promote trust and cooperation. Through these activities, readers develop relationship management skills, crucial for effective leadership.

Cultivating Emotional Intelligence in Leadership

The last section focuses on practical strategies for cultivating emotional intelligence in leadership. The section discusses mindfulness, self-reflection, and continuous learning as avenues for enhancing EI. You will practice the "Mindful Leadership Meditation," where they meditate on their leadership strengths and areas for improvement, fostering self-awareness and self-compassion. Through this practice, readers deepen their emotional intelligence, paving the way for impactful and empathetic leadership.

The Empathetic Leader

The conclusion emphasizes the transformative impact of emotional intelligence on leadership effectiveness and success. It reinforces that empathetic leadership is not just about skills but about embodying a culture of understanding, respect, and collaboration. You are encouraged to continue developing their emotional intelligence, knowing that through their empathetic leadership, they inspire and empower others, creating positive, inclusive, and high-performing work environments. Empathetic leaders, equipped with emotional intelligence, shape a future where compassion and understanding are at the heart of leadership.

5.2 INSPIRING AND MOTIVATING OTHERS: TECHNIQUES FOR EMOTIONALLY INTELLIGENT LEADERS TO INSPIRE AND MOTIVATE THEIR TEAMS.

"A good leader takes a little more than his share of the blame, a little less than his share of the credit." - Arnold H. Glasow

The focus shifts to the importance of recognition and appreciation in motivating teams. The section discusses the impact of genuine praise, acknowledgment, and celebrating achievements. You will engage in the "Appreciation Journal Exercise," where they regularly write down team members' achievements and qualities they appreciate. This practice enhances leaders' ability to recognize and appreciate their team, fostering a culture of positivity and motivation.

Coaching and Development: Inspiring Through Growth

This section explores the role of coaching and continuous development in motivating team members. You will learn about providing constructive feedback, setting growth-oriented goals, and offering learning opportunities. The section introduces the "Growth Mindset Workshop," where team members engage in activities promoting a growth mindset, embracing challenges, and learning from failures. Through this workshop, leaders inspire a culture of continuous learning and development, motivating their teams to achieve higher levels of performance.

Building a Positive Work Environment: Inspiring Through Positivity

The last section focuses on creating a positive and inclusive work environment that naturally motivates team members. The section discusses fostering collaboration, trust, and psychological safety. You will practice the "Positive Affirmation Circle," where team members share positive affirmations about one another. Through this practice, leaders create a culture of positivity and trust, motivating their teams to collaborate, innovate, and excel.

Conclusion: The Heartfelt Leader

The conclusion emphasizes the transformative impact of emotionally intelligent leadership in inspiring and motivating teams. It reinforces that genuine inspiration comes from understanding, appreciating, and connecting with team members on a human level. You are encouraged to continue practicing these techniques, knowing that through their empathetic and motivational leadership, they inspire their teams to achieve remarkable outcomes, fostering a workplace where people are not only productive but also fulfilled and motivated to contribute their best. The heartfelt leader, equipped with emotional intelligence, creates a work environment where inspiration and motivation are abundant, leading to shared success and fulfillment.

5.3 DECISION-MAKING AND EMOTIONAL INTELLIGENCE: UNDERSTANDING HOW EMOTIONAL INTELLIGENCE ENHANCES DECISION-MAKING PROCESSES AND OUTCOMES.

"Effective leadership is not about making speeches or being liked; leadership is defined by results, not attributes." - Peter Drucker

In this section, you will explore the intricate relationship between emotions and decision-making. The discussion emphasizes how emotions influence judgment, perception, and the decision-making process. The section introduces the "Emotional Decision Journal," encouraging readers to reflect on past decisions and identify the emotions involved. This practice initiates the journey toward understanding the impact of emotions on decision-making and the need for emotional intelligence in this process.

Self-Awareness and Decision-Making

This section delves into the role of self-awareness in making informed and mindful decisions. You will learn about recognizing personal biases, values, and emotional triggers. The section introduces the "Emotional Self-Reflection Exercise," guiding you to explore their emotional responses to various situations. Through this exercise, readers enhance self-awareness, enabling them to make decisions that align with their values and goals.

Emotional Regulation and Impulse Control

The focus shifts to emotional regulation and impulse control in decision-making. The section discusses techniques for managing stress, anxiety, and impulsive reactions. You will engage in the "Emotional Pause Technique," encouraging them to pause and breathe when faced with a decision, allowing time to assess emotions before responding. This practice enhances emotional regulation, leading to more thoughtful and rational decision-making.

Empathy and Decision-Making in Relationships

This section explores the role of empathy in decision-making, particularly in interpersonal relationships. You will learn how understanding others' perspectives can lead to better collaborative decisions. The section introduces the "Empathetic Decision Dialogue," where readers engage in a conversation with a colleague, considering each other's viewpoints before making a joint decision. Through this exercise, readers develop empathy, enhancing their ability to make decisions that consider the feelings and needs of others.

Social Skills and Decision-Making in Teams

The last section focuses on social skills and their impact on decision-making within teams and organizations. The section discusses effective communication, conflict resolution, and collaboration. You will practice the "Collaborative Decision-Making Simulation," where they work together in a simulated team project, making collective decisions. Through this simulation, readers enhance their social skills, fostering a collaborative decision-making environment within teams.

The Emotionally Intelligent Decision-Maker

The conclusion emphasizes the transformative power of emotional intelligence in decision-making processes and outcomes. It reinforces that emotionally intelligent decision-makers are aware of their emotions, regulate them effectively, empathize with others, and collaborate efficiently. You are encouraged to continue practicing emotional intelligence in their decision-making, knowing that through their awareness and empathy, they can make decisions that are not only rational but also compassionate, ethical, and inclusive. The emotionally intelligent decision-maker shapes a future where decisions are made with wisdom, empathy, and positive impact.

5.4 EMOTIONALLY INTELLIGENT COMMUNICATION: EFFECTIVE COMMUNICATION STRATEGIES FOR LEADERS TO FOSTER TRUST, COLLABORATION, AND ENGAGEMENT.

In this section, you will explore the fundamental principles of emotionally intelligent communication. The discussion emphasizes active listening, empathy, and understanding non-verbal cues. The section introduces the "Active Listening Circle," where readers practice attentive listening and respond empathetically to a partner's emotions. This exercise initiates the journey toward understanding the importance of emotional awareness in effective communication, setting the stage for building trust and collaboration.

Empathy in Communication

This section delves into the role of empathy in fostering meaningful connections through communication. You will learn how to identify and validate emotions in others, enhancing their ability to respond empathetically. The section introduces the "Empathy Role Play," where readers practice understanding and addressing emotions in various scenarios. Through this exercise, readers develop empathy skills, enabling them to connect with others on a deeper level and build trust in their interactions.

Conflict Resolution and Emotional Intelligence

The focus shifts to conflict resolution, highlighting the significance of emotional intelligence in navigating disagreements and misunderstandings. The section discusses de-escalation techniques, active listening during conflicts, and finding common ground. You will engage in the "Conflict Resolution Simulation," where they work through a conflict scenario using empathetic communication strategies. This simulation enhances readers‘ ability to manage conflicts with emotional intelligence, fostering understanding and collaboration.

Building Trust Through Emotional Communication

This section explores how emotionally intelligent communication builds trust within teams and organizations. The discussion includes transparency, authenticity, and vulnerability as key trust-building components. You will practice the "Trust-Building Circle," where team members share personal experiences and vulnerabilities, fostering trust and openness. Through this exercise, readers learn the power of authentic communication in establishing trust and creating a positive team environment.

Cultivating Engagement and Collaboration

The last section focuses on fostering engagement and collaboration through emotionally intelligent communication. The section discusses inclusive language, recognizing achievements, and appreciating diverse perspectives. You will engage in the "Collaborative Dialogue Workshop," where they participate in group discussions that encourage active listening and respectful exchange of ideas. Through this workshop, readers enhance their collaborative communication skills, creating an inclusive and engaged team culture.

Conclusion: The Emotionally Intelligent Communicator

The conclusion emphasizes the transformative impact of emotionally intelligent communication in leadership and team dynamics. It reinforces that emotionally intelligent communicators create environments where trust, collaboration, and engagement thrive. You are encouraged to continue practicing these communication strategies, knowing that through their empathetic and mindful communication, they foster connections, resolve conflicts, and inspire collaboration, leading to harmonious and high-performing teams. The emotionally intelligent communicator, equipped with empathy and understanding, paves the way for positive change and impactful leadership.

5.5 CREATING AN EMOTIONALLY INTELLIGENT WORKPLACE: PRACTICAL STEPS FOR LEADERS TO CREATE A CULTURE OF EMOTIONAL INTELLIGENCE WITHIN THEIR ORGANIZATIONS.

"The greatest ability in business is to get along with others and to influence their actions." - John Hancock

In this section, you will explore the importance of emotional intelligence (EI) in the workplace. The discussion emphasizes the impact of EI on teamwork, leadership, and organizational culture. The section introduces the "Emotional Intelligence Assessment," encouraging employees to assess their EI strengths and areas for development. This practice initiates the journey toward creating a workplace culture rooted in emotional intelligence.

Leadership and Emotional Intelligence

This section delves into the role of leadership in cultivating emotional intelligence within teams and organizations. You will learn how leaders can model EI, encourage open communication, and provide constructive feedback. The section introduces the "Leadership EI Workshop," where leaders engage in activities to enhance their EI skills. Through this workshop, leaders set an example for employees, fostering a culture of emotional intelligence from the top down.

Building Empathy and Collaboration

The focus shifts to building empathy and collaboration among team members. The section discusses the importance of understanding diverse perspectives, active listening, and resolving conflicts empathetically. You will engage in the "Empathy in Action Exercise," where teams work together to solve a challenge while actively listening and empathizing with each other. Through this exercise, employees enhance their empathetic and collaborative skills, creating a harmonious workplace environment.

Emotional Intelligence in Decision-Making

This section explores how emotional intelligence influences decision-making processes within the organization. The discussion includes making decisions based on empathy, understanding stakeholders' emotions, and considering long-term impacts. You will practice the "Decision-Making Simulation," where teams analyze a decision scenario from multiple emotional perspectives.

Through this simulation, employees learn to make more empathetic and thoughtful decisions, considering the emotional aspects of various stakeholders.

Cultivating a Positive Emotional Culture

The last section focuses on creating a positive emotional culture within the workplace. The section discusses the significance of gratitude, positivity, and recognition in fostering a supportive work environment. You will engage in the "Gratitude Circle," where employees share things, they are grateful for in their colleagues and workplace. Through this practice, employees cultivate a culture of appreciation and positivity, enhancing morale and well-being in the workplace.

The Emotionally Intelligent Workplace

The conclusion emphasizes the transformative impact of creating an emotionally intelligent workplace. It reinforces that an emotionally intelligent workplace fosters trust, collaboration, and employee well-being. Leaders and employees are encouraged to continue practicing emotional intelligence, knowing that through their empathetic and mindful approach, they contribute to a workplace where employees thrive, conflicts are resolved peacefully, and creativity and innovation flourish. The emotionally intelligent workplace becomes a space where people are not just productive but also happy, fulfilled, and connected to their work and colleagues.

CHAPTER SEVEN

EMOTIONAL INTELLIGENCE IN CONFLICT RESOLUTION

"Peace is not absence of conflict, it is the ability to handle conflict by peaceful means." - Ronald Reagan

In the heart of a fervent protest, amidst heated emotions and charged conversations, Mahatma Gandhi stood as a beacon of emotional intelligence. Once, during a particularly tense meeting, an agitated man approached him, hurling insults and threats. Instead of reacting with anger or retaliation, Gandhi calmly acknowledged the man's feelings.

With unwavering composure, Gandhi listened intently to the man's grievances, acknowledging his pain and frustration. He responded not with hostility, but with empathy, understanding the deep-rooted emotions behind the man's anger. In that moment, Gandhi's emotional intelligence shone brightly. He recognized the humanity in his opponent, even in the face of conflict.

With genuine empathy, Gandhi spoke softly, addressing the man's concerns and fears. He used words infused with understanding and compassion, slowly diffusing the tension in the room. By acknowledging the emotions at play and responding with empathy, Gandhi turned a potential confrontation into a dialogue. In that transformative moment, he showcased the power of emotional intelligence in resolving conflicts, leaving behind a legacy of peaceful resolution through understanding and compassion.

Conflict is an inevitable part of life, and how we manage it can greatly impact our relationships and overall well-being. In this section, we will explore the role of emotional intelligence in conflict resolution, highlighting its importance and providing practical strategies to navigate conflicts effectively.

Figure:19

Understanding Emotional Intelligence

Emotional intelligence (EI) refers to our ability to recognize, understand, and manage our own emotions, as well as empathize with others. It encompasses self-awareness, self-regulation, social awareness, and relationship management. By developing emotional intelligence, we can enhance our conflict resolution skills and foster healthier interactions.

The Impact of Emotions in Conflict

Emotions play a significant role in conflicts, often intensifying the situation and clouding rational thinking. Unmanaged emotions can lead to hostility, misunderstandings, and breakdowns in communication. Emotional intelligence equips us with the tools to effectively manage our emotions, de-escalate conflicts, and find mutually beneficial resolutions.

Building Self-Awareness

Self-awareness is the foundation of emotional intelligence. It involves recognizing our own emotions, triggers, and patterns of behavior. By developing self-awareness, we can better understand our reactions during conflicts and take steps to regulate our emotions. Techniques such as mindfulness, journaling, and self-reflection can help to cultivate self-awareness.

Empathy and Perspective-Taking

Empathy is a key component of emotional intelligence and a powerful tool in conflict resolution. It involves understanding and sharing the feelings of others. By actively listening, putting ourselves in the shoes of the other person, and seeking to understand their perspective, we can foster empathy and create a more empathetic and compassionate approach to conflict resolution.

Section 5: Effective Communication and Active Listening

Clear and effective communication is essential in resolving conflicts. Emotional intelligence enables us to communicate assertively, expressing our needs and concerns while also actively listening to the other person. Active listening involves giving our full attention, seeking clarification, and validating the emotions and experiences of others. By practicing active listening, we create a safe and open space for dialogue, promoting understanding and resolution.

Conclusion:

In conclusion, emotional intelligence plays a vital role in conflict resolution. By developing self-awareness, empathy, and effective communication skills, we can navigate conflicts with greater understanding, empathy, and respect. Cultivating emotional intelligence allows us to transform conflicts into opportunities for growth, understanding, and strengthened relationships.

6.1 UNDERSTANDING CONFLICT: EXPLORING THE NATURE OF CONFLICTS AND THEIR IMPACT ON RELATIONSHIPS.

"The best way to destroy an enemy is to make him a friend." - Abraham Lincoln

In this section, you will explore the fundamental nature of conflicts, including their triggers, escalation, and resolution. The discussion emphasizes understanding the several types of conflicts and their impact on relationships. The section introduces the "Conflict Diary," encouraging readers to journal their conflicts, identifying emotions, triggers, and resolutions. This practice initiates the journey toward understanding the root causes of conflicts and their dynamics.

Emotional Intelligence in Conflict Resolution

This section delves into the role of emotional intelligence (EI) in resolving conflicts effectively. You will learn about self-awareness, empathy, and active listening as key components of EI during conflicts. The section introduces the "Empathetic Response Exercise," where readers practice responding to a conflict scenario with empathy and understanding. Through this exercise, readers enhance their EI skills, enabling them to navigate conflicts with emotional intelligence.

Communication Patterns in Conflict

The focus shifts to communication patterns that contribute to conflicts. The section discusses assertive communication, non-verbal cues, and active listening as essential skills in conflict resolution. You will engage in the "Active Listening Role Play," where they practice active listening and assertive communication in pairs. Through this role play, readers develop effective communication techniques, fostering understanding and resolving conflicts more peacefully.

Conflict Resolution Strategies

This section explores various conflict resolution strategies, including negotiation, compromise, and collaboration. You will learn when to apply each strategy based on the nature of the conflict. The section introduces the "Collaborative Problem-Solving Workshop," where readers work together to find solutions to a frequent problem. This workshop enhances readers' collaborative skills, encouraging them to find win-win solutions to conflicts.

Mediation and Conflict Transformation

The last section focuses on mediation and conflict transformation techniques. The section discusses the role of neutral mediators, active listening, and reframing in transforming conflicts into opportunities for growth. You will practice the "Conflict Transformation Meditation," where they visualize a conflict transforming into a peaceful resolution. Through this meditation, readers develop a mindset of transforming conflicts into opportunities for understanding, learning, and strengthening relationships.

Conclusion: Embracing Conflict as an Opportunity for Growth

The conclusion emphasizes the transformative potential of conflicts in relationships. It reinforces those conflicts, when approached with empathy, emotional intelligence, and effective communication, can lead to deeper understanding and stronger connections. You are encouraged to view conflicts as opportunities for growth, self-reflection, and improved communication. By embracing conflicts as natural aspects of relationships and applying the skills learned, readers can navigate conflicts constructively, fostering healthier, more resilient relationships.

6.2 EMOTIONAL INTELLIGENCE AND CONFLICT RESOLUTION: APPLYING EMOTIONAL INTELLIGENCE PRINCIPLES TO EFFECTIVELY RESOLVE CONFLICTS AND PROMOTE HARMONY.

"When you talk, you are only repeating what you already know. But if you listen, you may learn something new." - Dalai Lama

In this section, you will explore the core principles of emotional intelligence (EI) and its impact on conflict resolution. The discussion emphasizes self-awareness, empathy, and emotional regulation as essential EI components in resolving conflicts. The section introduces the "Emotional Self-Reflection Journal," encouraging readers to reflect on their emotional responses in past conflicts. This practice initiates the journey toward understanding the role of emotions in conflicts and the application of EI for resolution.

Developing Empathetic Communication Skills

This section delves into the importance of empathetic communication in resolving conflicts effectively. You will learn active listening techniques, recognizing non-verbal cues, and validating emotions. The section introduces the "Empathetic Listening Exercise," where readers practice listening to a partner's concerns and responding empathetically. Through this exercise, readers enhance their empathetic communication skills, fostering a deeper understanding of others' perspectives.

Emotional Regulation in Conflict Situations

The focus shifts to emotional regulation and impulse control during conflicts. The section discusses techniques for managing anger, frustration, and impulsive reactions. You will engage in the "Emotional Regulation Breathing Exercise," encouraging them to practice deep breathing and mindfulness techniques during conflict situations. This exercise enhances emotional control, allowing readers to respond thoughtfully rather than react impulsively during conflicts.

Mediation and Conflict Transformation

This section explores mediation techniques and conflict transformation strategies grounded in emotional intelligence. The discussion includes reframing perspectives, finding common ground, and facilitating dialogue. You will practice the "Conflict Transformation Visualization," where they visualize a conflict situation transforming into a peaceful resolution. Through this visualization, readers develop a mindset of transformation and harmony, encouraging creative solutions to conflicts.

Building a Culture of Emotional Intelligence in Teams

The last section focuses on fostering a culture of emotional intelligence within teams and organizations. The section discusses the role of leadership, training programs, and open communication in promoting EI among team members. You will engage in the "Team Building EI Workshop," where team members participate in activities that promote emotional intelligence, such as trust-building exercises and empathetic communication simulations. Through this workshop, teams cultivate emotional intelligence collectively, creating a harmonious and supportive work environment.

Embracing Emotional Intelligence for Lasting Harmony

The conclusion emphasizes the transformative impact of applying emotional intelligence principles to conflict resolution. It reinforces that embracing emotional intelligence not only resolves conflicts effectively but also promotes lasting harmony and positive relationships. You are encouraged to continue practicing emotional intelligence in their interactions, knowing that through their empathetic understanding, emotional regulation, and open communication, they can create workplaces and relationships where conflicts are opportunities for growth and understanding. The emotionally intelligent approach to conflict resolution becomes a cornerstone for creating a more empathetic, understanding, and harmonious world.

6.3 ACTIVE LISTENING IN CONFLICT RESOLUTION: UTILIZING ACTIVE LISTENING SKILLS TO UNDERSTAND DIFFERENT PERSPECTIVES AND FIND COMMON GROUND.

"Most people do not listen with the intent to understand; they listen with the intent to reply." - Stephen R. Covey

In this section, you will delve into the foundational principles of active listening and its pivotal role in conflict resolution. The discussion emphasizes the art of truly hearing others, fostering empathy, and creating a safe space for open dialogue. The section introduces the "Reflective Listening Practice," encouraging readers to paraphrase what they have heard to ensure understanding. This practice initiates the journey toward mastering active listening techniques for resolving conflicts effectively.

Empathy in Active Listening

This section explores the deep connection between empathy and active listening. You will learn how empathetic listening fosters emotional understanding, creating a conducive environment for conflict resolution. The section introduces the "Empathy Mapping Exercise," where readers map out the emotions they perceive in a speaker's words and body language. Through this exercise, readers enhance their ability to empathize, creating bridges of understanding even in challenging conversations.

Overcoming Barriers to Active Listening

The focus shifts to identifying and overcoming common barriers to active listening. The section discusses distractions, biases, and emotional triggers that hinder effective listening. You will engage in the "Mindful Listening Meditation," where they practice focusing on sounds and sensations mindfully. This meditation enhances concentration and mindfulness, empowering readers to overcome distractions and listen attentively in conflict situations.

Applying Active Listening in Different Contexts

This section explores the diverse applications of active listening in various contexts, including personal relationships, professional settings, and community interactions. You will learn how adapting active listening techniques to different situations can lead to more meaningful connections. The section introduces the "Role-

Play Scenarios," where readers practice active listening in simulated real-life situations. Through these role-plays, readers gain practical experience in applying active listening skills contextually.

Active Listening for Lasting Resolution

The last section focuses on utilizing active listening skills for sustainable conflict resolution. The section discusses active listening as a tool for finding common ground, building trust, and fostering collaboration. You will engage in the "Conflict Resolution Workshop," where they participate in guided discussions, actively listen to conflicting parties, and facilitate resolution-oriented dialogues. Through this workshop, readers hone their active listening skills, equipping themselves to resolve conflicts and build enduring relationships.

Conclusion: The Heart of Harmonious Relationships

The conclusion emphasizes the transformative impact of active listening on relationships and conflict resolution. It reinforces that active listening is not merely a skill but a way of being present and understanding others deeply. You are encouraged to continue practicing active listening, knowing that through their empathetic and attentive listening, they can foster understanding, resolve conflicts, and build bridges of harmony in all aspects of their lives. The art of active listening becomes a cornerstone for building a world where compassion, empathy, and mutual respect reign, leading to more profound connections and peaceful coexistence.

6.4 MANAGING ANGER AND FRUSTRATION: TECHNIQUES FOR MANAGING ANGER AND FRUSTRATION IN CONFLICT SITUATIONS FOR CONSTRUCTIVE RESOLUTION.

"He who angers you conquers you." - Elizabeth Kenny

In this section, you will explore the nature of anger and frustration, understanding their triggers and the impact they have on conflict situations. The discussion emphasizes self-awareness and emotional regulation as essential skills. The section introduces the "Anger Journaling Exercise," encouraging readers to journal their anger triggers and responses. This practice initiates the journey toward understanding the root causes of anger and frustration, paving the way for constructive resolution techniques.

Emotional Regulation Strategies

This section delves into various strategies for emotional regulation, including deep breathing, mindfulness, and cognitive reframing. You will learn how these techniques can help manage anger and frustration effectively. The section introduces the "Mindful Breathing Exercise," guiding you to focus on their breath to calm their minds during heated moments. Through this exercise, readers develop emotional regulation skills, enabling them to respond thoughtfully rather than react impulsively in conflict situations.

Assertive Communication Techniques

The focus shifts to assertive communication as a tool for managing anger and frustration constructively. The section discusses techniques such as "I" statements and active listening to express emotions effectively. You will engage in the "Role-Play Scenario," where they practice assertive communication in simulated conflict situations. Through these role-plays, readers enhance their assertiveness skills, allowing them to express their feelings without escalating the conflict.

Empathy and Perspective-Taking

This section explores how empathy and perspective-taking can diffuse anger and frustration during conflicts.

You will learn how understanding others' viewpoints can lead to more compassionate responses. The section introduces the "Empathy Walk Exercise," where readers mentally put themselves in the shoes of the other person to understand their perspective. Through this exercise, readers develop empathy, enabling them to approach conflicts with understanding and empathy.

Transformative Conflict Resolution

The last section focuses on transformative conflict resolution techniques that go beyond managing anger and frustration to finding mutually beneficial solutions. The section discusses collaborative problem-solving, compromise, and finding common ground. You will engage in the "Conflict Transformation Workshop," where they work in pairs to find creative solutions to a conflict scenario. Through this workshop, readers enhance their critical thinking skills, fostering a spirit of collaboration and understanding in conflict resolution.

Conclusion: A Path to Constructive Resolution

The conclusion emphasizes the transformative journey from managing anger and frustration to constructive conflict resolution. It reinforces that by understanding the roots of anger, regulating emotions, practicing assertive communication, and cultivating empathy, individuals can navigate conflicts effectively. You are encouraged to continue practicing these techniques, knowing that through their mindful and empathetic approach, they can transform conflicts into opportunities for growth, understanding, and strengthened relationships. Managing anger and frustration becomes not just a skill but a way of fostering harmony, leading to more meaningful connections and peaceful resolutions.

6.5 FORGIVENESS AND HEALING: EXPLORING THE ROLE OF FORGIVENESS IN CONFLICT RESOLUTION AND THE HEALING PROCESS.

"Forgiveness does not change the past, but it does enlarge the future." - Paul Boese

Forgiveness is a profound and transformative act that holds the potential to mend broken relationships, resolve conflicts, and facilitate personal healing. In this section, we will explore the role of forgiveness in conflict resolution and the overall healing process. By delving into the importance of forgiveness, understanding its benefits, and exploring practical strategies for embracing forgiveness, we can unlock the transformative power it holds.

Understanding Forgiveness

Forgiveness is a complex and multifaceted concept that goes beyond merely pardoning someone's actions. It involves a shift in perspective, a willingness to let go of resentment, and a choice to release the emotional burden associated with the transgression. By acknowledging that forgiveness does not condone the wrongdoer's actions, but rather sets the forgiver free from the negative emotions that bind them, we can begin to grasp its true essence.

The Benefits of Forgiveness

Forgiveness brings an array of benefits to both the forgiver and the forgiven. Research has shown that practicing forgiveness leads to reduced stress levels, improved mental and emotional well-being, enhanced self-esteem, and increased overall life satisfaction. Additionally, forgiveness fosters empathy, compassion, and the potential for reconciliation, thereby paving the way for healthier and more harmonious relationships.

Embracing Forgiveness in Conflict Resolution

Conflict is an inevitable part of human interactions, and forgiveness plays a pivotal role in resolving conflicts constructively. By embracing forgiveness, individuals can shift their focus from blame and resentment towards understanding, empathy, and finding common ground. It allows for open dialogue, a willingness to listen, and the possibility of finding mutually beneficial solutions. Forgiveness creates an environment conducive to healing wounds, rebuilding trust, and fostering long-term peace.

Practical Strategies for Cultivating Forgiveness

Cultivating forgiveness requires conscious effort and practice. One effective strategy is developing empathy by putting ourselves in the shoes of the person who has wronged us. This helps us gain a deeper understanding of their motivations and experiences. Another approach is reframing the narrative, focusing on personal growth and the lessons learned from the experience. Engaging in self-reflection, seeking professional help if needed, and practicing self-compassion are also valuable tools in the journey towards forgiveness.

Conclusion:

In conclusion, forgiveness holds immense power in conflict resolution and the healing process. By understanding its essence, embracing its benefits, and employing practical strategies, we can foster personal growth, mend broken relationships, and create a more harmonious world. Let us remember that forgiveness is not a sign of weakness, but rather a courageous act of self-liberation and compassion. Together, let us embark on a journey of forgiveness and healing.

CHAPTER EIGHT

EMBRACING EMOTIONAL INTELLIGENCE IN EVERYDAY LIFE

"The greatest glory in living lies not in never falling, but in rising every time we fall." - Nelson Mandela

In a fast-paced and demanding world, embracing emotional intelligence can be the key to cultivating a fulfilling and balanced life. Understanding our emotions, empathizing with others, and effectively communicating are vital skills that can positively impact our relationships, decision-making, and overall well-being. In this sectiont, we will explore the importance of emotional intelligence and how to incorporate it into our everyday lives.

What is Emotional Intelligence?

Emotional intelligence, often referred to as EQ, is the ability to recognize, understand, and manage our own emotions and the emotions of others. It encompasses self-awareness, self-regulation, empathy, and effective social skills. By developing emotional intelligence, we enhance our capacity for self-reflection, empathy, and resilience.

The Benefits of Emotional Intelligence

Embracing emotional intelligence offers numerous benefits. Firstly, it enables us to navigate conflicts and challenges with greater ease, fostering healthier relationships. Additionally, emotional intelligence enhances our decision-making abilities, as we can make rational choices while considering the emotional impact on ourselves and others. Moreover, it contributes to personal well-being, reducing stress levels and promoting mental and emotional balance.

Cultivating Emotional Intelligence in Everyday Life

a) Self-Awareness: The foundation of emotional intelligence lies in self-awareness. Take time to reflect on your own emotions, triggers, and patterns of behavior. Journaling or mindfulness practices can be helpful tools for developing self-awareness.

b) Empathy: Practice putting yourself in someone else's shoes. Actively listen and seek to understand their perspectives and emotions. Showing empathy fosters deeper connections and strengthens relationships.

c) Emotional Regulation: Learn to identify and manage your own emotions in healthy ways. Engage in activities that promote emotional well-being, such as exercise, meditation, or engaging in hobbies that bring you joy.

d) Effective Communication: Enhance your communication skills by expressing yourself clearly and assertively. Pay attention to non-verbal cues and listen actively. Effective communication promotes understanding and reduces misunderstandings.

Conclusion:

Embracing emotional intelligence is a transformative journey that can impact our lives. By nurturing self-awareness, empathy, emotional regulation, and effective communication, we can cultivate deeper connections, make wiser decisions, and experience greater overall well-being. Let us embrace emotional intelligence and embark on a path towards a more balanced and fulfilling life.

7.1 EMOTIONAL INTELLIGENCE IN THE WORKPLACE: APPLYING EMOTIONAL INTELLIGENCE SKILLS TO ENHANCE PRODUCTIVITY, COLLABORATION, AND JOB SATISFACTION.

"The best and most beautiful things in the world cannot be seen or even touched. They must be felt with the heart." - Helen Keller

In today's fast-paced and competitive workplace, emotional intelligence has emerged as a crucial skill set for professionals across various industries. By understanding and managing our own emotions and effectively navigating the emotions of others, we can enhance productivity, foster collaboration, and experience greater job satisfaction. This section will explore the importance of emotional intelligence in the workplace and provide practical ways to apply emotional intelligence skills for a thriving work environment.

Understanding Emotional Intelligence

Emotional intelligence, often referred to as EQ, encompasses a range of skills including self-awareness, self-regulation, empathy, and social skills. It involves recognizing and understanding our emotions, as well as those of others, and leveraging them to build stronger relationships and make more informed decisions. By developing emotional intelligence, individuals can effectively manage conflicts, adapt to change, and cultivate positive workplace dynamics.

Enhancing Productivity through Self-Awareness and Self-Regulation

One key aspect of emotional intelligence is self-awareness, which involves recognizing our own emotions, strengths, and weaknesses. By being aware of our emotional triggers and patterns, we can consciously regulate our responses and make more rational choices. This self-awareness allows us to manage stress, maintain focus, and improve our overall productivity. Additionally, self-regulation enables us to handle criticism constructively and bounce back from setbacks, fostering a resilient and solution-oriented work environment.

Building Empathy for Effective Collaboration

Empathy, another vital component of emotional intelligence, enables us to understand and share the feelings of others. In the workplace, empathy plays a crucial role in fostering effective collaboration and teamwork. By actively listening to colleagues, acknowledging their perspectives, and demonstrating empathy, we create an inclusive and supportive atmosphere. This not only strengthens interpersonal relationships but also enhances cooperation, creativity, and innovation within teams.

Cultivating Social Skills for Positive Work Relationships

Social skills encompass a range of abilities such as communication, conflict resolution, and networking. These skills are essential for building positive work relationships and creating a harmonious work environment. By honing our social skills, we can effectively express our ideas, provide constructive feedback, and resolve conflicts amicably. Strong social skills also enable us to build professional networks, establish rapport with colleagues, and foster a sense of camaraderie within the workplace.

Conclusion:

Emotional intelligence serves as a powerful tool for success in the modern workplace. By cultivating self-awareness, self-regulation, empathy, and social skills, professionals can unlock their full potential and create a positive work environment. Applying emotional intelligence skills results in enhanced productivity, improved collaboration, and increased job satisfaction. As we continue to prioritize emotional intelligence in the workplace, we pave the way for greater success, both individually and collectively.

7.2 EMOTIONAL INTELLIGENCE IN PERSONAL RELATIONSHIPS: CULTIVATING EMOTIONAL INTELLIGENCE IN PERSONAL RELATIONSHIPS FOR DEEPER CONNECTIONS AND FULFILLMENT.

"To love and be loved is to feel the sun from both sides." - David Viscott

In this section, you will explore the core elements of emotional intelligence (EI) and their significance in personal relationships. The discussion emphasizes self-awareness, empathy, and effective communication as essential components of EI. The section introduces the "Emotional Self-Reflection Exercise," encouraging readers to assess their emotional triggers and responses in various relationship scenarios. This practice initiates the journey toward understanding the role of EI in building meaningful connections.

Empathy and Active Listening in Relationships

This section delves into the role of empathy and active listening in fostering deep emotional connections. You will learn the art of utterly understanding their partners‘ emotions and expressing genuine empathy. The section introduces the "Empathy Circle Exercise," where partners take turns sharing their feelings and practicing active listening. Through this exercise, couples enhance their empathetic communication skills, creating a foundation for emotional intimacy.

Conflict Resolution and Emotional Intelligence

The focus shifts to conflict resolution within relationships, emphasizing the importance of emotional regulation and understanding during disagreements. The section discusses techniques for managing emotions, reframing perspectives, and finding compromises. You will engage in the "Conflict Resolution Role-Play," where they practice resolving a hypothetical conflict using EI techniques. Through this role-play, couples develop conflict resolution skills, promoting harmony and understanding in their relationships.

Emotional Intelligence in Intimate Relationships

This section explores the unique dynamics of intimate relationships and how emotional intelligence contributes to intimacy and passion. The discussion includes vulnerability, trust-building, and maintaining emotional connection. You will participate in the "Intimacy Building Ritual," where partners engage in a mindful and intimate activity, fostering emotional closeness. Through this ritual, couples deepen their emotional bond, creating a more fulfilling and passionate relationship.

Nurturing Emotional Intelligence Together

The last section focuses on cultivating emotional intelligence as a partnership. The section discusses collaborative goal setting, supporting each other's emotional growth, and creating a shared emotional language. You will engage in the "Emotional Support Practice," where partners identify each other's emotional needs and work together to fulfill them. Through this practice, couples create a supportive emotional environment, encouraging each other's personal and relational growth.

Conclusion: The Joy of Deep Emotional Connections

The conclusion emphasizes the transformative power of emotional intelligence in personal relationships. It reinforces that by practicing self-awareness, empathy, active listening, and effective communication, couples can create profound emotional connections and lasting fulfillment. You are encouraged to continue cultivating emotional intelligence in their relationships, knowing that through their conscious efforts, they can build a relationship filled with understanding, love, and genuine emotional intimacy. Emotional intelligence becomes not just a skill but a way of nurturing relationships that bring joy, support, and deep fulfillment.

7.3 EMOTIONAL INTELLIGENCE AND PARENTING: APPLYING EMOTIONAL INTELLIGENCE PRINCIPLES TO RAISE EMOTIONALLY INTELLIGENT AND RESILIENT CHILDREN.

"Children have never been very good at listening to their elders, but they have never failed to imitate them." - James Baldwin

In this section, you will delve into the core principles of emotional intelligence (EI) and its vital role in effective parenting. The discussion emphasizes self-awareness, empathy, and emotional regulation as key components of EI. The section introduces the "Parental Self-Reflection Exercise," encouraging parents to assess their own emotional responses and triggers. This practice initiates the journey toward applying EI principles in raising emotionally intelligent and resilient children.

Nurturing Emotional Literacy in Children

This section explores the development of emotional literacy in children, focusing on recognizing, understanding, and expressing emotions. Parents will learn strategies to help their children label and manage their feelings effectively. The section introduces the "Emotion Recognition Game," where parents and children identify emotions in facial expressions and discuss situations related to those emotions. Through this game, children enhance their emotional vocabulary and understanding, fostering emotional intelligence.

Teaching Emotional Regulation and Coping Skills

The focus shifts to emotional regulation and coping skills, essential for children's resilience. The section discusses techniques such as deep breathing, mindfulness, and positive self-talk. Parents and children will engage in the "Calm Down Corner Activity," creating a designated space where children can practice calming techniques when upset. Through this activity, children develop emotional regulation skills, empowering them to handle challenging situations with composure.

Building Empathy and Social Skills

This section explores the development of empathy and social skills in children, emphasizing the importance of perspective-taking and kindness. Parents will learn activities to encourage empathy, such as storytelling and role-playing. The section introduces the "Empathy Storytelling Exercise," where parents and children create stories from different characters' perspectives, promoting understanding of diverse emotions and experiences. Through this exercise, children develop empathy and social intelligence, fostering positive relationships with others.

Strengthening Parent-Child Connections

The last section focuses on strengthening the parent-child bond through emotional connection and trust. The section discusses active listening, validating feelings, and spending quality time together. Parents and children will engage in the "Gratitude Journaling Activity," where they write down things, they appreciate about each other daily. Through this activity, families cultivate gratitude, enhancing positive emotions and strengthening their emotional connection.

Conclusion: Raising Emotionally Intelligent and Resilient Children

The conclusion emphasizes the transformative impact of applying emotional intelligence principles in parenting. It reinforces that by nurturing emotional intelligence, parents empower their children to navigate the complexities of emotions, relationships, and challenges with resilience and empathy. Parents are encouraged to continue practicing these principles, knowing that through their guidance, understanding, and support, they are fostering emotionally intelligent and resilient individuals who will thrive in all aspects of life. Emotional intelligence becomes the cornerstone for building strong, loving, and emotionally intelligent families.

7.4 EMOTIONAL INTELLIGENCE AND WELL-BEING: EXPLORING HOW EMOTIONAL INTELLIGENCE CONTRIBUTES TO OVERALL WELL-BEING AND MENTAL HEALTH.

"Happiness is not something ready-made. It comes from your own actions." - Dalai Lama XIV

In this section, you will explore the intricate relationship between emotional intelligence (EI) and mental well-being. The discussion emphasizes the impact of EI on managing stress, building resilience, and fostering positive emotions. The section introduces the "Emotional Check-In Exercise," encouraging readers to assess their current emotional state and its impact on their overall well-being. This practice initiates the journey toward understanding how EI contributes to mental health and overall life satisfaction.

Emotional Regulation and Stress Management

This section delves into the role of emotional regulation in managing stress and promoting mental well-being. You will learn practical techniques such as mindfulness, deep breathing, and positive reframing. The section introduces the "Mindful Breathing Meditation," guiding readers through a calming breathing exercise. Through this meditation, readers enhance their emotional regulation skills, enabling them to cope with stress and anxiety effectively.

Building Resilience Through Emotional Intelligence

The focus shifts to resilience-building strategies grounded in emotional intelligence. The section discusses reframing setbacks, cultivating a growth mindset, and practicing self-compassion. You will engage in the "Resilience Journaling Exercise," where they reflect on past challenges, their emotional responses, and the lessons learned. Through journaling, readers enhance their resilience, developing a positive outlook and the ability to bounce back from adversities.

Cultivating Positive Relationships and Emotional Well-Being

This section explores how EI contributes to the quality of relationships and emotional well-being. The discussion includes empathetic communication, active listening, and conflict resolution skills. You will participate in the "Empathy Circle Activity," where they practice empathetic listening and sharing within a group. Through this activity, readers enhance their empathetic abilities, fostering deeper connections and emotional fulfillment in their relationships.

Enhancing Self-Compassion and Life Satisfaction

The last section focuses on the practice of self-compassion and its impact on overall life satisfaction. The section discusses self-acceptance, self-kindness, and embracing imperfections. You will engage in the "Loving-Kindness Self-Compassion Exercise," where they send wishes of love and kindness to themselves. Through this exercise, readers cultivate self-compassion, nurturing a positive self-image and enhancing their overall sense of well-being.

Conclusion: Embracing Emotional Intelligence for a Fulfilling Life

The conclusion emphasizes the transformative power of emotional intelligence on mental well-being and overall life satisfaction. It reinforces that by honing emotional intelligence skills, individuals can navigate life's challenges with grace, foster positive relationships, and cultivate a deep sense of fulfillment. You are encouraged to continue practicing these principles, knowing that through their emotional intelligence, they can create a life rich in meaning, joy, and emotional well-being. Emotional intelligence becomes the cornerstone for a fulfilling and balanced life.

7.5 CREATING A POSITIVE IMPACT: HARNESSING EMOTIONAL INTELLIGENCE TO CREATE A POSITIVE IMPACT ON ONESELF AND OTHERS IN VARIOUS LIFE SCENARIOS.

"You must be the change you wish to see in the world." - Mahatma Gandhi

In this section, you will explore the concept of positive impact and how emotional intelligence (EI) serves as a catalyst for creating positive change. The discussion emphasizes the importance of empathy, understanding, and compassion in making a difference. The section introduces the "Gratitude Journaling Exercise," encouraging readers to reflect on the positive impacts they have experienced or witnessed. This practice initiates the journey toward understanding the role of EI in fostering positivity and kindness.

Positive Impact in Personal Relationships

This section delves into how emotional intelligence can enhance personal relationships, fostering understanding, trust, and harmony. You will learn about empathetic communication, active listening, and conflict resolution skills. The section introduces the "Positive Communication Challenge," where readers practice expressing themselves positively even in challenging conversations. Through this challenge, readers enhance their communication skills, promoting positivity and creating a harmonious atmosphere in their relationships.

Positive Impact in the Workplace

The focus shifts to the professional sphere, exploring how EI can create a positive impact in the workplace. The section discusses empathetic leadership, effective teamwork, and conflict resolution strategies. You will engage in the "Empathy in Leadership Workshop," where they participate in role-playing scenarios to practice empathetic leadership skills. Through this workshop, readers enhance their leadership abilities, fostering a positive work environment and encouraging the professional growth of their team members.

Positive Impact in Community and Society

This section explores how emotional intelligence can drive positive change in communities and society at large. The discussion includes active citizenship, social empathy, and collaborative problem-solving. You will participate in the "Community Impact Project," where they identify a local issue, collaborate with others, and implement a solution using empathetic and emotionally intelligent approaches. Through this project, readers contribute positively to their community, highlighting the transformative power of EI in creating social change.

Sustainable Positive Impact

The last section focuses on sustaining positive impact over time. The section discusses self-care, resilience, and mindful living as essential components of maintaining a positive and empathetic approach in various life scenarios. You will engage in the "Mindful Living Challenge," where they practice incorporating mindfulness into their daily routines. Through this challenge, readers enhance their emotional resilience, ensuring that their positive impact efforts are sustainable and enduring.

Becoming Agents of Positive Change

The conclusion emphasizes the potential within every individual to become an agent of positive change through emotional intelligence. It reinforces that by cultivating empathy, understanding, and kindness, individuals can create a ripple effect of positivity in their personal lives, relationships, workplaces, and communities. You are encouraged to continue practicing these principles, knowing that through their emotionally intelligent actions, they can contribute to a more compassionate and harmonious world. Emotional intelligence becomes the driving force for transformative and sustainable positive impact, leaving a legacy of kindness and empathy.

CHAPTER NINE

CONCLUSION

8.1 REFLECTING ON THE JOURNEY: ENCOURAGING READERS TO REFLECT ON THEIR PERSONAL GROWTH AND TRANSFORMATION THROUGHOUT THE BOOK.

"The journey of a thousand miles begins with one step." - Lao Tzu

In this opening section, you are introduced to the concept of self-reflection and its significance in personal growth and transformation. The discussion emphasizes self-awareness, mindfulness, and the value of looking inward. The section includes the "Self-Reflection Journal Exercise," where You are encouraged to begin their self-reflection journey by journaling their thoughts and feelings. This practice initiates the process of exploring one's personal growth throughout the book.

Unpacking Emotional Intelligence

This section delves into the core principles of emotional intelligence and its role in personal development. You will learn about self-awareness, empathy, and emotional regulation. The section includes the "Emotional Self-Discovery Exercise," where readers assess their current emotional intelligence and identify areas for improvement. Through this exercise, readers set the stage for their personal growth and transformation.

Navigating Self-Discovery

The focus shifts to the journey of self-discovery, including challenges, setbacks, and moments of enlightenment. The section discusses the importance of resilience, learning from failures, and embracing vulnerability. You will engage in the "Embracing Vulnerability Journaling Exercise," where they reflect on times when they embraced vulnerability and how it contributed to their personal growth. This exercise encourages readers to explore their own transformative moments.

Cultivating Emotional Resilience

This section explores the development of emotional resilience and its role in navigating life's challenges. The discussion includes coping strategies, self-compassion, and positive reframing. You will participate in the "Resilience Building Meditation," where they practice a guided meditation focused on building emotional resilience. Through this meditation, readers enhance their ability to bounce back from setbacks and continue their personal growth journey.

The Journey Continues

The last section reflects on the entire self-discovery journey. It emphasizes the idea that self-reflection is an ongoing process and encourages readers to continue their personal growth and transformation. The section includes the "Continued Self-Reflection Exercise," where readers set goals for their ongoing self-reflection practice and commit to their personal development journey.

Conclusion: Embracing Your Transformation

The conclusion of the book reinforces the idea that personal growth and transformation are ongoing processes. It encourages readers to celebrate their progress and highlights the importance of self-reflection as a tool for continuous development. You are reminded that their self-reflection journey does not end with the book but continues as a lifelong practice, leading to greater self-awareness and personal growth. Self-reflection becomes a powerful tool for embracing and nurturing one's own transformation.

8.2 EMBRACING EMOTIONAL MASTERY: SUMMARIZING THE KEY TAKEAWAYS AND EMPHASIZING THE IMPORTANCE OF CONTINUED PRACTICE AND GROWTH IN EMOTIONAL INTELLIGENCE.

"Education is the kindling of a flame, not the filling of a vessel." - Socrates

In this opening section, you are introduced to the core principles of emotional mastery. The discussion emphasizes self-awareness, self-regulation, and empathy as foundational skills. The section includes the "Emotional Awareness Practice," where readers observe their emotions without judgment for a few minutes each day. This practice initiates the process of building self-awareness, a fundamental step toward emotional mastery.

Cultivating Self-Regulation

This section delves into the practice of self-regulation and emotional balance. You will learn techniques such as deep breathing, mindfulness, and reframing negative thoughts. The section includes the "Mindful Breathing Exercise," guiding readers through a calming breathing practice. Through this exercise, readers enhance their ability to regulate their emotions, promoting a sense of calm and centeredness.

Mastering Empathy and Compassion

The focus shifts to empathy and compassion, essential components of emotional mastery. The section discusses active listening, understanding others‘ perspectives, and practicing random acts of kindness. You will participate in the "Empathy in Action Challenge," where they perform small acts of kindness for others and observe the impact on their own emotions. Through this challenge, readers enhance their empathy and compassion, fostering deeper connections with others.

Building Resilience and Adaptability

This section explores the development of resilience and adaptability in the face of challenges. The discussion includes reframing setbacks, learning from failures, and embracing change. You will engage in the "Resilience Visualization Exercise," where they visualize themselves overcoming a challenging situation with grace and resilience. Through this visualization, readers enhance their ability to bounce back from adversities, fostering emotional strength.

Sustaining Emotional Mastery

The last section focuses on sustaining emotional mastery over time. It discusses the integration of emotional intelligence into daily life, maintaining a growth mindset, and fostering positive habits. You will participate in the "Daily Emotional Mastery Ritual," where they set aside a few minutes each day for self-reflection, gratitude, and intention setting. Through this ritual, readers ensure that their emotional mastery practice becomes a consistent and integral part of their lives.

Conclusion: Embracing a Lifetime of Emotional Mastery

The conclusion emphasizes that emotional mastery is a lifelong journey of self-discovery and growth. It encourages readers to celebrate their progress while acknowledging that there is always room for further development. You are reminded that emotional mastery is not a destination but a continuous process of self-improvement. The conclusion encourages readers to commit to their emotional intelligence practice, knowing that by embracing emotional mastery, they are not only enhancing their own well-being but also positively influencing the lives of those around them. Emotional mastery becomes a guiding principle for a life filled with resilience, empathy, and meaningful connections.

8.3 CREATING A FUTURE OF EMOTIONAL INTELLIGENCE: INSPIRING READERS TO APPLY THEIR NEWFOUND EMOTIONAL INTELLIGENCE SKILLS TO CREATE A BETTER FUTURE FOR THEMSELVES AND THOSE AROUND THEM.

"Your life does not get better by chance, it gets better by change." - Jim Rohn

In this opening section, you are encouraged to visualize a future where emotional intelligence (EI) is a guiding force in their lives and society. The discussion emphasizes the positive impact of EI on relationships, workplaces, and communities. The section includes the "Future Self Visualization," where readers imagine their future selves applying EI skills in various scenarios. This practice initiates the process of setting intentions for a future filled with emotional intelligence.

Emotional Intelligence in Relationships

This section delves into how EI can transform relationships. You will learn about empathetic communication, conflict resolution, and fostering emotional intimacy. The section includes the "Compassionate Communication Exercise," where readers practice expressing their feelings and needs with empathy.

Through this exercise, readers enhance their relationship skills, creating a future where understanding and compassion are at the core of their interactions.

Emotional Intelligence in Leadership

The focus shifts to the impact of EI in leadership and professional environments. The section discusses empathetic leadership, effective teamwork, and fostering a positive work culture. You will participate in the "Leadership Vision Board Activity," where they create a visual representation of their ideal workplace environment guided by emotional intelligence principles. Through this activity, readers envision a future workplace where EI drives decision-making and collaboration.

Emotional Intelligence in Education

This section explores the integration of EI into educational systems. The discussion includes teaching empathy, emotional regulation, and conflict resolution skills to students. You will engage in the "Empathy in Education Workshop," where they design a curriculum or activity to promote empathy among students. Through this workshop, readers contribute to a future where emotional intelligence is nurtured from an early age, shaping compassionate and empathetic generations.

Building Emotionally Intelligent Communities

The last section focuses on creating emotionally intelligent communities and societal structures. The discussion includes active citizenship, social empathy, and collective problem-solving. You will participate in the "Community EI Initiative," where they plan a project or initiative that promotes emotional intelligence within their community. Through this initiative, readers actively contribute to a future where EI is valued, understood, and practiced on a larger scale.

Conclusion: Empowering a Future of Emotional Intelligence

The conclusion emphasizes the transformative power of applying emotional intelligence skills to shape a better future. It reinforces that each reader has the potential to create positive change in their personal lives, relationships, workplaces, and communities. You are encouraged to take consistent, small actions guided by EI principles, knowing that these actions collectively contribute to a future where empathy, understanding, and emotional intelligence are the norm rather than the exception. Emotional intelligence becomes a beacon guiding you toward a future where compassion, kindness, and emotional awareness create a harmonious and empathetic world.

8.4 ACKNOWLEDGMENTS: EXPRESSING GRATITUDE TO THOSE WHO HAVE SUPPORTED AND CONTRIBUTED TO THE BOOK'S CREATION.

"In the end, it is important to remember that we cannot become what we need to be by remaining what we are." - Max DePree

In this opening section, you are introduced to the concept of gratitude and its profound impact on well-being. The discussion emphasizes the importance of expressing gratitude for the people, experiences, and lessons in our lives. The section includes the "Daily Gratitude Journal," encouraging readers to write down three things they are grateful for each day. This practice initiates the journey toward cultivating a mindset of gratitude, fostering positivity and appreciation.

Acknowledging Supportive Relationships

This section delves into the significance of acknowledging and appreciating the supportive relationships in our lives. You will learn about the power of expressing gratitude to friends, family, colleagues, and mentors. The section includes the "Gratitude Letter Exercise," where readers write a heartfelt letter to someone who has supported them. Through this exercise, readers strengthen their connections and express genuine appreciation, deepening their relationships.

Gratitude in Challenging Times

The focus shifts to the practice of gratitude during inconvenient situations. The section discusses finding positive aspects, learning from hardships, and acknowledging the strength within. You will engage in the "Gratitude Amidst Challenges Meditation," where they reflect on a challenging situation and identify aspects to be thankful for. Through this meditation, readers develop resilience and a positive perspective, even in the face of adversity.

Gratitude for Personal Growth

This section explores the role of gratitude in personal growth and self-discovery. The discussion includes acknowledging one's own strengths, achievements, and moments of growth. You will participate in the "Self-Appreciation Exercise," where they list their qualities, accomplishments, and personal growth experiences. Through this exercise, readers boost their self-esteem and self-compassion, recognizing their worth and potential.

Spreading Gratitude to the World

The last section focuses on the ripple effect of gratitude, inspiring readers to spread gratitude to others and the world. The section discusses acts of kindness, volunteering, and contributing to the community. You will engage in the "Gratitude in Action Challenge," where they perform random acts of kindness for strangers or volunteer their time to a charitable cause. Through this challenge, readers actively contribute to creating a more grateful and compassionate world.

Conclusion: The Continuous Journey of Gratitude

The conclusion emphasizes that the practice of gratitude is not just a one-time exercise but a lifelong journey. It encourages readers to continue expressing gratitude, fostering positive relationships, and contributing to the well-being of others. You are reminded that gratitude is a transformative force, shaping their perspective, relationships, and overall quality of life. By embracing gratitude as a way of being, readers create a cycle of positivity and kindness, enriching their lives and the lives of those around them. Gratitude becomes a guiding principle, illuminating the path toward a fulfilling and appreciative existence.

8.5 RESOURCES FOR FURTHER GROWTH: PROVIDING ADDITIONAL RESOURCES AND RECOMMENDATIONS FOR READERS TO CONTINUE THEIR JOURNEY OF EMOTIONAL INTELLIGENCE.

"The best way to predict the future is to create it." - Abraham Lincoln

Emotional intelligence plays a crucial role in our personal and professional lives, impacting our relationships, decision-making abilities, and overall well-being. To help you further develop and enhance your emotional intelligence skills, we have curated a list of valuable resources and recommendations. Whether you are just starting your journey or seeking to deepen your understanding, these resources will provide guidance and support along the way.

Books for Emotional Intelligence

Reading is a fantastic way to expand your knowledge and gain insights into emotional intelligence. Here are three highly recommended books to consider:

1. "Emotional Intelligence" by Daniel Goleman: This groundbreaking book explores the concept of emotional intelligence and its significance in our lives. Goleman provides practical strategies to develop self-awareness, empathy, and social skills.

2. "Emotional Agility" by Susan David: David's book offers transformative insights on how to navigate our emotions effectively and adapt to the ever-changing world. She provides powerful tools to build resilience, embrace change, and thrive in challenging situations.

3. "The Language of Emotions" by Karla McLaren: In this book, McLaren delves into the rich world of emotions, guiding you to understand and honor their emotions. She offers tools for healthier emotional expression, communication, and relationships.

Online Courses and Workshops

If you prefer interactive learning experiences, online courses and workshops can be an excellent choice. Here are three reputable platforms that offer valuable resources on emotional intelligence:

1. Coursera: Explore courses like "The Science of Well-Being" by Yale University or "Leading with Emotional Intelligence" by Case Western Reserve University. These courses provide in-depth knowledge and practical strategies to enhance emotional intelligence.

2. Emotional Intelligence Training Company: This organization offers online workshops and training programs specifically focused on emotional intelligence development. Their courses cover various aspects, including self-awareness, empathy, and effective communication.

3. LinkedIn Learning: Access a wide range of courses on emotional intelligence, such as "Building Emotional Intelligence" by Gemma Leigh Roberts or "Developing Your Emotional Intelligence" by Britt Andreatta. These courses provide valuable insights and actionable techniques to improve emotional intelligence skills.

Podcasts for Emotional Intelligence

Podcasts offer a convenient way to learn on the go. Here are three recommended podcasts that explore emotional intelligence:

1. "The Science of Happiness": Produced by the Greater Good Science Center at UC Berkeley, this podcast explores the science behind happiness, well-being, and emotional intelligence. It features inspiring stories, expert interviews, and practical tips.

2. "Happier with Gretchen Rubin": In this podcast, bestselling author Gretchen Rubin and her sister Elizabeth Craft share insights and strategies for creating a happier life. They discuss diverse topics related to emotional intelligence, habits, and personal growth.

3. "The EQ Evolution": Hosted by emotional intelligence coach and author Anabel Jensen, this podcast explores different facets of emotional intelligence in various contexts. It provides tools, interviews, and stories to support personal and professional growth.

Conclusion:

Emotional intelligence is a lifelong journey that can enhance our relationships, well-being, and success. By immersing ourselves in resources like books, online courses, workshops, and podcasts, we can continue to cultivate our emotional intelligence skills. Remember, practice and self-reflection are key to unlocking the full potential of emotional intelligence.

In the final pages of "Embracing Emotional Intelligence," You are reminded of the transformative journey they have undertaken. The book, rooted in the principles of self-awareness, empathy, and emotional regulation, has guided them through the intricate pathways of understanding and mastering their emotions. It is within these emotions that readers have discovered the profound power of connection, resilience, and personal growth.

"Embracing Emotional Intelligence" begins by laying the foundation, introducing readers to the core concepts of emotional intelligence and its pivotal role in personal and professional success. Through engaging narratives, practical exercises, and real-life examples, readers learn to recognize, understand, and manage their emotions effectively. The book explores the nuances of empathy, compassion, and self-reflection, guiding you toward nurturing healthier relationships and a more profound sense of self.

The sections unfold a comprehensive exploration of emotional intelligence, from self-awareness and self-regulation to empathetic communication and resilience. Through mindful exercises and actionable practices, you are empowered to apply these principles in their daily lives, fostering emotional well-being and harmonious connections with others.

Throughout the book, the importance of continuous growth and learning is emphasized. You are encouraged to view emotional intelligence not as a destination but as an enriching journey. By integrating the lessons and practices shared in this book, you are equipped to navigate life's challenges with grace, understanding, and emotional mastery.

CHAPTER TEN

APPENDIX 1: SELF ASSESSMENT

Emotional Intelligence Self-Assessment:

Below is a detailed self-assessment on Emotional Intelligence (EI) divided into four major types: Self-Awareness, Self-Management, Social Awareness, and Relationship Management. Each type contains set of questions to help individuals evaluate their emotional intelligence skills. Participants are encouraged to rate themselves on a scale from 1 to 5, where:

Type 1: Self-Awareness

Emotional intelligence self-assessment helps you to become more self-aware. It allows you to recognize your own emotions, understand why you feel a certain way, and how your emotions affect your thoughts and behavior.

I am aware of my own emotions even in stressful situations.

☐Strongly Disagree ☐Disagree ☐Neutral ☐Agree ☐ Strongly Agree

I can identify the emotions I am feeling and understand why I am feeling them.

☐Strongly Disagree ☐Disagree ☐Neutral ☐Agree ☐ Strongly Agree

I recognize how my emotions influence my thoughts and behavior.

☐Strongly Disagree ☐Disagree ☐Neutral ☐Agree ☐ Strongly Agree

I understand my strengths and weaknesses and how they impact my relationships.

☐Strongly Disagree ☐Disagree ☐Neutral ☐Agree ☐ Strongly Agree

I can accurately assess my abilities and limitations.

☐Strongly Disagree ☐Disagree ☐Neutral ☐Agree ☐ Strongly Agree

I am aware of my values, beliefs, and their impact on my decisions.

☐Strongly Disagree ☐Disagree ☐Neutral ☐Agree ☐ Strongly Agree

I am open to feedback, even if it is critical.

☐Strongly Disagree ☐Disagree ☐Neutral ☐Agree ☐ Strongly Agree

I can acknowledge my mistakes and learn from them.

☐Strongly Disagree ☐Disagree ☐Neutral ☐Agree ☐ Strongly Agree

I understand my emotional triggers and can manage them effectively.

☐Strongly Disagree ☐Disagree ☐Neutral ☐Agree ☐ Strongly Agree

I regularly reflect on my emotions and behavior to gain insights into myself.

☐Strongly Disagree ☐Disagree ☐Neutral ☐Agree ☐ Strongly Agree

I can articulate my feelings and thoughts clearly to others.

☐Strongly Disagree ☐Disagree ☐Neutral ☐Agree ☐ Strongly Agree

I am comfortable with my emotions and do not feel the need to suppress them.

☐Strongly Disagree ☐Disagree ☐Neutral ☐Agree ☐ Strongly Agree

I can sense the emotional atmosphere in a room even without words being spoken.

☐Strongly Disagree ☐Disagree ☐Neutral ☐Agree ☐ Strongly Agree

I am aware of how my emotions affect those around me.

☐Strongly Disagree ☐Disagree ☐Neutral ☐Agree ☐ Strongly Agree

I am open to exploring new aspects of my personality and emotions.

☐Strongly Disagree ☐Disagree ☐Neutral ☐Agree ☐ Strongly Agree

Type 2: Self-Management

Emotional intelligence self-assessment helps in recognizing stress triggers and understanding how stress affects emotions. With this awareness, you can develop effective stress management strategies, leading to improved overall well-being.

I can control impulsive reactions, even in challenging situations.

☐Strongly Disagree ☐Disagree ☐Neutral ☐Agree ☐ Strongly Agree

I manage my stress levels effectively and have healthy coping mechanisms.

☒Strongly Disagree ☐Disagree ☐Neutral ☐Agree ☐ Strongly Agree

I am proactive in seeking personal and professional growth.

☐Strongly Disagree ☐Disagree ☐Neutral ☐Agree ☐ Strongly Agree

I can adapt to change and remain calm in uncertain situations.

☐Strongly Disagree ☐Disagree ☐Neutral ☐Agree ☐ Strongly Agree

I am resilient and bounce back quickly from setbacks.

☐Strongly Disagree ☐Disagree ☐Neutral ☐Agree ☐ Strongly Agree

I set realistic goals for myself and work steadily towards achieving them.

☒Strongly Disagree ☐Disagree ☐Neutral ☐Agree ☐ Strongly Agree

I can delay gratification and resist temptations when necessary.

☐Strongly Disagree ☐Disagree ☐Neutral ☐Agree ☐ Strongly Agree

I practice mindfulness and stay present in the moment.

☐Strongly Disagree ☐Disagree ☐Neutral ☐Agree ☐ Strongly Agree

I effectively manage my time and prioritize tasks.

☐Strongly Disagree ☐Disagree ☐Neutral ☐Agree ☐ Strongly Agree

I am open to trying innovative approaches and am not afraid of failure.

☐Strongly Disagree ☐Disagree ☐Neutral ☐Agree ☐ Strongly Agree

I maintain a healthy work-life balance.

☐Strongly Disagree ☐Disagree ☐Neutral ☐Agree ☐ Strongly Agree

I do not let negative emotions affect my decision-making process.

☐Strongly Disagree ☐Disagree ☐Neutral ☐Agree ☐ Strongly Agree

I am able to handle criticism without feeling overly defensive.

☐Strongly Disagree ☐Disagree ☐Neutral ☐Agree ☐ Strongly Agree

I am adaptable to changing circumstances without losing my composure.

☐Strongly Disagree ☐Disagree ☐Neutral ☐Agree ☐ Strongly Agree

I am proactive in resolving personal issues and conflicts.

☐Strongly Disagree ☐Disagree ☐Neutral ☐Agree ☐ Strongly Agree

Type 3: Social Awareness

Emotional intelligence self-assessment helps you to gain insights into your own thoughts, emotions and behaviors, which in turn can lead a better understanding of how they interact with others and how they are perceived in social situations.

I can accurately perceive others‘ emotions by their facial expressions and body language.

☐Strongly Disagree ☐Disagree ☐Neutral ☐Agree ☐ Strongly Agree

I actively listen when others are speaking and show genuine interest in their perspective.

☐Strongly Disagree ☐Disagree ☐Neutral ☐Agree ☐ Strongly Agree

I am sensitive to the feelings and needs of others in a group setting.

☒Strongly Disagree ☐Disagree ☐Neutral ☐Agree ☐ Strongly Agree

I can identify the social dynamics in a room and adapt my behavior accordingly.

☐Strongly Disagree ☐Disagree ☐Neutral ☐Agree ☐ Strongly Agree

I am empathetic and can understand others' emotions from their point of view.

☐Strongly Disagree ☐Disagree ☐Neutral ☐Agree ☐ Strongly Agree

I respect diverse viewpoints and appreciate diverse cultural perspectives.

☐Strongly Disagree ☐Disagree ☐Neutral ☐Agree ☐ Strongly Agree

I can recognize when someone is feeling upset, even if they do not express it directly.

☐Strongly Disagree ☐Disagree ☐Neutral ☐Agree ☐ Strongly Agree

I can sense the emotional atmosphere in a group and respond appropriately.

☐Strongly Disagree ☐Disagree ☐Neutral ☐Agree ☐ Strongly Agree

I can pick up on non-verbal cues and understand their significance in communication.

☐Strongly Disagree ☐Disagree ☐Neutral ☐Agree ☐ Strongly Agree

I am aware of the social norms in different situations and cultures.

☐Strongly Disagree ☐Disagree ☐Neutral ☐Agree ☐ Strongly Agree

Type 4: Relationship Management

Emotional intelligence is crucial in interpersonal relationships. Assessing one's emotional intelligence helps in understanding how emotions impact interactions with others. It enables you to respond empathetically, handle conflicts better, and build healthier relationships.

I can resolve conflicts effectively and find solutions that satisfy all parties involved.

☐Strongly Disagree ☐Disagree ☐Neutral ☐Agree ☐ Strongly Agree

I am skilled at giving constructive feedback without hurting others' feelings.

☐Strongly Disagree ☐Disagree ☐Neutral ☐Agree ☐ Strongly Agree

I can inspire and influence others positively.

☐Strongly Disagree ☐Disagree ☐Neutral ☐Agree ☐ Strongly Agree

I am adept at building rapport with people from various backgrounds.

☐Strongly Disagree ☐Disagree ☐Neutral ☐Agree ☐ Strongly Agree

I can mediate in disagreements and help parties find common ground.

☐Strongly Disagree ☐Disagree ☐Neutral ☐Agree ☐ Strongly Agree

I am supportive and encouraging of others' goals and aspirations.

☐Strongly Disagree ☐Disagree ☐Neutral ☐Agree ☐ Strongly Agree

I can handle difficult conversations with tact and diplomacy.

☐Strongly Disagree ☐Disagree ☐Neutral ☐Agree ☐ Strongly Agree

I can negotiate effectively, finding solutions that are acceptable to all parties.

☐Strongly Disagree ☐Disagree ☐Neutral ☐Agree ☐ Strongly Agree

I can maintain a balance between assertiveness and empathy in my interactions.

☐Strongly Disagree ☐Disagree ☐Neutral ☐Agree ☐ Strongly Agree

I can lead a team with emotional intelligence, fostering collaboration and trust.

☐Strongly Disagree ☐Disagree ☐Neutral ☐Agree ☐ Strongly Agree

Scoring:

Total your scores for each type of Emotional Intelligence separately. The maximum possible score for each type is 75 (15 questions x 5 points each). Interpret your scores to understand your strengths and areas for improvement within each type of Emotional Intelligence. Remember that this assessment is meant for self-reflection and personal development. Use your results as a starting point for enhancing your emotional intelligence skills.

After completing the Emotional Intelligence self-assessment and obtaining your scores, you can use the results to gain valuable insights into your emotional intelligence strengths and areas for improvement. Here is what you can do with your self-assessment scores and the next steps you might consider:

1. Reflect on Your Scores:

Identify Strengths: Acknowledge the areas where you scored high. These are your emotional intelligence strengths. Recognizing these strengths can boost your confidence and affirm your existing capabilities.

Recognize Areas for Improvement: Take note of the areas where your scores were lower. These indicate aspects of emotional intelligence that might require more attention and development.

2. Understand the Implications:

Personal Relationships: Reflect on how your emotional intelligence impacts your personal relationships. Consider how improved self-awareness and empathy might enhance your interactions with family and friends.

Professional Environment: Think about your workplace interactions. Emotional intelligence is crucial for leadership, teamwork, conflict resolution, and effective communication in the workplace.

3. Set Goals:

Short-Term Goals: Identify specific, achievable goals to improve your emotional intelligence. For example, you could set a goal to actively listen to others without judgment or practice stress-reduction techniques.

Long-Term Goals: Consider long-term goals, such as building stronger relationships, becoming a more effective leader, or enhancing your overall well-being through emotional intelligence.

4. Seek Resources:

Books and Articles: Explore literature on emotional intelligence. There are numerous books and articles that provide practical insights and techniques for developing emotional intelligence.

Workshops and Courses: Consider attending workshops or online courses focused on emotional intelligence. These provide structured learning experiences and often include interactive exercises.

5. Practice Mindfulness:

Self-Reflection: Regularly reflect on your emotional responses and behaviors. Mindful self-reflection can enhance self-awareness, a fundamental aspect of emotional intelligence.

Mindfulness Meditation: Consider incorporating mindfulness meditation into your routine. It can help you stay present, manage stress, and improve your overall emotional well-being.

6. Seek Feedback:

Ask for Feedback: Seek feedback from friends, family, or colleagues about your emotional intelligence. Their perspectives might provide valuable insights that you may not have considered.

7. Monitor Your Progress:

Regular Check-Ins: Periodically reassess your emotional intelligence using self-assessment tools. Track your progress over time to see how your scores evolve as you work on enhancing your emotional intelligence skills.

8. Be Patient and Persistent:

Patience: Developing emotional intelligence is a journey that takes time and consistent effort. Be patient with yourself as you work on improving your skills.

Persistency: Consistency is key. Make emotional intelligence development a continuous part of your personal and professional growth.

Remember, enhancing your emotional intelligence can lead to improved relationships, better communication, and increased overall well-being. Stay committed to your development, and you will likely find that it positively impacts various aspects of your life.

CHAPTER ELEVEN

APPENDIX 2: SUMMARY OF THE BOOK

n the tapestry of human experience, Emotional Intelligence threads the needle, weaving together empathy, self-awareness, and social understanding. This book, a guiding light, unravels the intricate layers of our emotions, fostering compassion, resilience, and meaningful connections. As we embrace our own emotional landscape, we navigate relationships with wisdom and grace. Through self-reflection and empathy, we embark on a transformative journey toward profound emotional mastery. The pages of this book echo with the wisdom that emotional intelligence is not just a skill; it is the very essence of a fulfilling and harmonious life.

Aspect	Description	Action Steps
Self-Awareness	Understanding your own emotions and recognizing their impact on your thoughts and behavior.	1. Practice mindfulness meditation to increase self-awareness. 2. Keep a journal to track your emotions and reactions.
Self-Management	Managing your emotions effectively, especially in challenging situations. Developing healthy coping mechanisms and resilience.	1. Identify stress triggers and practice relaxation techniques. 2. Learn time management skills to reduce overwhelming situations.
Social Awareness	Empathizing with others, understanding their emotions, and navigating social dynamics. Being culturally sensitive and perceptive to non-verbal cues.	1. Engage in active listening during conversations. 2. Participate in cultural events to broaden your perspective. 3. Practice reading body language.
Relationship Management	Building and maintaining healthy relationships, resolving conflicts, and effective communication. Fostering teamwork and collaboration.	1. Develop active communication skills, both verbal and non-verbal. 2. Practice assertiveness without aggression. 3. Participate in team-building activities.

Table:2

Aspect	Description	Action Steps
Empathy	Understanding others' emotions and perspectives, being sensitive to their feelings, and demonstrating compassion.	1. Engage in perspective-taking exercises to understand others' viewpoints. 2. Volunteer for community service to enhance empathy.
Conflict Resolution	Effectively resolving disagreements and finding mutually beneficial solutions. Managing disagreements with tact and diplomacy.	1. Practice active listening and paraphrasing to ensure mutual understanding. 2. Take a conflict resolution workshop to enhance skills.
Influence	Positively impacting others, inspiring and motivating them, and being persuasive without manipulation.	1. Develop storytelling skills to make your messages more compelling. 2. Learn negotiation techniques to influence decisions positively.
Resilience	Bouncing back from setbacks, learning from failures, and adapting to change.	1. Develop a growth mindset through affirmations and positive self-talk. 2. Practice mindfulness to handle stress and build emotional resilience.
Leadership Skills	Leading with emotional intelligence, fostering a positive work environment, and empowering others.	1. Attend leadership training programs to enhance your leadership skills. 2. Mentor others and provide constructive feedback for growth.

Table:3

CHAPTER TWELVE

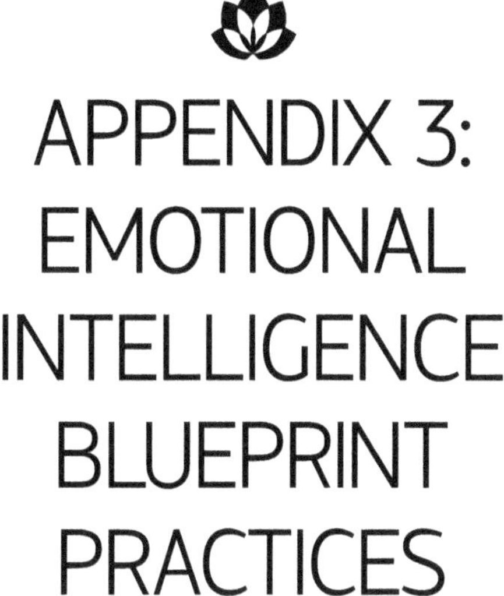

APPENDIX 3: EMOTIONAL INTELLIGENCE BLUEPRINT PRACTICES

Emotional Intelligence Blueprint Practices:

The Emotional Intelligence Blueprint Practices aim to empower individuals with essential skills to enhance their emotional intelligence. Through a structured approach, these practices facilitate self-awareness, empathy, and effective interpersonal interactions. The blueprint covers various aspects of emotional intelligence, including self-awareness, self-management, social awareness, and relationship management.

Instructions: Implement the following practices to enhance your Emotional Intelligence skills.

Page 1: Self-Awareness	Description	Action Steps
Practice 1	**Mindful Reflection:** Regularly reflect on your emotions and reactions.	1. Set aside 10 minutes daily for mindful self-reflection. 2. Journal your thoughts and emotions.
Practice 2	**Emotion Identification:** Develop your vocabulary for emotions.	1. Learn about different emotions and their subtle nuances. 2. Practice identifying emotions in others.

Table:4

Page 2: Self-Management	Description	Action Steps
Practice 1	**Stress Management:** Implement stress-reducing techniques.	1. Practice deep breathing exercises during stressful situations. 2. Exercise regularly to release tension.
Practice 2	**Time Management:** Enhance your time management skills.	1. Prioritize tasks and create a daily to-do list. 2. Set realistic goals and deadlines.

Table:5

Page 3: Social Awareness	Description	Action Steps
Practice 1	**Empathetic Listening:** Practice active and empathetic listening.	1. Maintain eye contact and nod to show understanding. 2. Validate others' feelings during conversations.
Practice 2	**Cultural Sensitivity:** Increase your awareness of cultural differences.	1. Read about various cultures and their customs. 2. Engage with diverse communities and learn from their experiences.

Table:6

Page 4: Relationship Management	Description	Action Steps
Practice 1	**Effective Communication:** Enhance your verbal and non-verbal communication.	1. Practice active listening by paraphrasing what others say. 2. Improve your body language to appear open and approachable.
Practice 2	**Conflict Resolution:** Develop skills to resolve conflicts peacefully.	1. Use "I" statements to express your feelings without blaming others. 2. Seek compromises that satisfy all parties involved.

Table:7

Page 5: Empathy and Compassion	**Description**	**Action Steps**
Practice 1	**Empathy Exercises:** Engage in exercises to enhance empathy.	1. Put yourself in others' shoes by imagining their feelings. 2. Volunteer for charitable causes to connect with others' struggles.
Practice 2	**Compassionate Acts:** Perform small acts of kindness regularly.	1. Help a colleague with their tasks without expecting anything in return. 2. Donate to a charity and actively participate in community service.

Table:8

This format provides a systematic breakdown of practices for each aspect of Emotional Intelligence. Readers can refer to the specific pages relevant to the skills you want to enhance. Feel free to customize the practices and expand on each action step based on your specific audience and the depth of guidance you intend to provide.

Final Thoughts:

In the closing words of "Embracing Emotional Intelligence," You are invited to embrace the full spectrum of your emotions, acknowledging them as valuable messengers guiding them toward a more fulfilling life. The book concludes by expressing gratitude for the reader's dedication to their emotional growth and reminds them that the journey of emotional intelligence is boundless, offering endless opportunities for self-discovery, meaningful connections, and a life enriched by the depth of human emotions. Armed with newfound emotional intelligence, you are prepared to embark on a future filled with resilience, empathy, and a profound understanding of the intricate tapestry of human emotions.

Graditude For Readers

Dear Esteemed Readers,

I pen down these words with a heart brimming with gratitude and humility. As the author of "Emotional Alchemy: Guide to Boost your EQ Skills" I want to express my heartfelt thanks to each one of you who embarked on this transformative journey within the pages of this book.

Authoring this book was a labor of love, and your presence on this expedition has given it purpose and meaning. Your dedication to exploring the depths of emotional intelligence, your willingness to engage with the exercises, and your openness to embracing change have inspired me beyond measure.

I am profoundly thankful for your trust in the wisdom shared within these sections. Your commitment to understanding and mastering your emotions not only enriches your life but contributes to a more empathetic and compassionate world. Your efforts to cultivate emotional intelligence ripple outward, touching the lives of those around you, fostering understanding, and nurturing harmonious relationships.

Remember, the journey of emotional intelligence is not confined to the pages of this book; it is a lifelong odyssey. I encourage you to continue exploring, learning, and growing. Each step you take in this direction not only enhances your own well-being but also adds to the collective emotional intelligence of humanity.

Once again, thank you for your time, your energy, and your dedication. May your newfound wisdom in emotional intelligence guide you toward a future filled with profound self-awareness, genuine connections, and a deep sense of fulfillment.

With heartfelt gratitude,

Elangovan Radhakrishnan - Author

ISBN - 978-93-6012-975-0

www.ingramcontent.com/pod-product-compliance
Lightning Source LLC
LaVergne TN
LVHW021153160826
845679LV00024B/2110

* 9 7 9 8 8 9 1 8 6 1 7 3 2 *